DK Pocket Genius

ANCIENT EGYPT

FACTS AT YOUR FINGERTIPS

DK DELHI
Project editor Virien Chopra
Art editors Vikas Chauhan, Pooja Pawwar
Senior editor Samira Sood
Senior art editor Govind Mittal
Assistant editor Jubbi Francis
DTP designers Arvind Kumar,
Jaypal Singh Chauhan
Picture researcher Sumedha Chopra

DK LONDON
Senior editor Rob Houston
Senior art editor Philip Letsu
US editor Margaret Parrish
Jacket editor Manisha Majithia
Jacket designer Laura Brim
Jacket manager Amanda Lunn
Production editor Rebekah Parsons-King
Production controller Mary Slater
Publisher Andrew Macintyre
Associate publishing director Liz Wheeler
Art director Phil Ormerod
Publishing director Jonathan Metcalf
Consultant John Haywood

TALL TREE LTD.
Editors Rob Colson, Joe Fullman, Jon Richards
Art editor Ed Simkins

First American Edition, 2012
This edition published in the United States in 2016 by
DK Publishing, 345 Hudson Street, New York, New York 10014

A catalog record for this book
is available from the Library of Congress.
ISBN: 978-1-4654-4524-7

DK books are available at special discounts when purchased in
bulk for sales promotions, premiums, fund-raising, or educational
use. For details, contact: DK Publishing Special Markets,
345 Hudson Street, New York, New York 10014
SpecialSales@dk.com

Printed and bound in China

A WORLD OF IDEAS:
SEE ALL THERE IS TO KNOW

www.dk.com

CONTENTS

Scales and sizes

This book contains profiles of Egyptian buildings, monuments, and artifacts, with scale drawings to indicate their size.

1,063 ft (324 m)   6 ft (1.8 m)   6 in (15 cm)

Geo-locator
The location of a temple is marked as a red dot on this map of Egypt.

Gold bracelet of Sheshonq II

The Nile River

For 5,000 years, the Nile River has been the focus of Egyptian life. Many of the cities and monuments of ancient Egypt, shown below, were built along the banks of the river, the main source of water in this arid region.

One of the oldest cities in ancient Egypt, **Heliopolis** was also the center of worship of many gods.

Each of **the three pyramids** at Giza had temples as well as pyramids for wives and mothers. The Sphinx belongs to the middle pyramid. Officials were buried nearby in a separate area.

Mediterranean Sea

Alexandria

LOWER EGYPT

Bubastis

Heliopolis
Cairo

Giza

Saqqara

Memphis

Meidum

Herakleopolis

Hermopolis

Beni Hasan

Akhetaten (Amarna)

Sahara

Red Sea

Sinai Peninsula

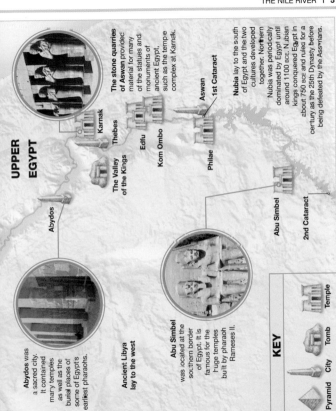

UPPER EGYPT

Abydos was a sacred city. It contained many temples as well as the burial places of some of Egypt's earliest pharaohs.

Ancient Libya lay to the west

Abu Simbel was located at the southern border of Egypt. It is famous for the huge temples built by pharaoh Rameses II.

The stone quarries of Aswan provided material for many of the statues and monuments of ancient Egypt, such as the temple complex at Karnak.

Nubia lay to the south of Egypt and the two cultures developed together. Northern Nubia was periodically dominated by Egypt until around 1100 BCE. Nubian kings conquered Egypt in about 750 BCE and ruled for a century as the 25th Dynasty before being defeated by the Assyrians.

Karnak

Thebes

The Valley of the Kings

Abydos

Edfu

Kom Ombo

Philae

Aswan

1st Cataract

Abu Simbel

2nd Cataract

KEY

Pyramid   City   Tomb   Temple

History of ancient Egypt

"Ancient Egypt" is the period between about 3500 BCE and 30 BCE, when Egypt was ruled by dynasties of pharaohs. Historians divide this stretch of time into three main periods of prosperity—the Old, Middle, and New Kingdoms. The periods in between and after the kingdoms were times of unrest.

Predynastic Period

The Egyptians began to farm in about 5500 BCE and formed settled communities. It took about 2,000 years for regional kings to appear. By c. 3100 BCE these regions had merged into one state.

Ram-shaped palette used to grind minerals for eye paint

3500 BCE	3250 BCE	3000 BCE	2750 BCE
Pre-dynastic Period		**Early Dynastic Period**	

Early Dynastic Period

Around 3100 BCE, all of Egypt was unified under one rule. The first ruler of the 1st Dynasty was Narmer. In this New Kingdom tomb painting the god Horus wears the double crown. The crown symbolized the unification of Egypt.

Tomb model of beer-brewing, c.2160 BCE

Middle Kingdom

About 2055 BCE, Egypt was unified under Mentuhotep II of the 11th Dynasty, marking the beginning of the Middle Kingdom. At first under local princes, control was gradually reformed to strengthen a central government. National boundaries were guarded and pushed south into Nubia, a source of gold.

First Intermediate Period

During this period, power was divided between the 9th and 10th Dynasties, which ruled Lower Egypt from Herakleopolis, and the 11th Dynasty, which ruled Upper Egypt from Thebes.

2500 BCE	2250 BCE		2000 BCE	1750 BCE
Old Kingdom	First Intermediate Period		Middle Kingdom	

Old Kingdom

Also known as the "Age of the Pyramids," the Old Kingdom was the period in which ancient Egypt's greatest monuments were built, such as the pyramids of Giza and the Great Sphinx. Egypt became a strong and prosperous kingdom in this period. The Old Kingdom ended around 2160 BCE, and the central control of the Egyptian state broke apart.

Pyramids of Giza

Second Intermediate Period

The 15th Dynasty, known as the Hyksos, originated from the Levant and for a short period ruled all of Egypt. This Dynasty was finally defeated by Theban kings at the end of the 17th and beginning of the 18th Dynasties.

Nubian pyramid, built around 700–300 BCE

Model boat from the burial of Ahhotep, a 17th Dynasty queen

1750 BCE	1500 BCE	1250 BCE	1000 BCE
Second Intermediate Period	New Kingdom		Third Intermediate Period

New Kingdom

Lasting from 1550–1086 BCE, the New Kingdom is considered to be the greatest period in the history of ancient Egypt. Strong rulers, such as Ahmose I and Thutmose III, expanded the influence of Egypt both south and north. This time also saw the building of numerous temples and monuments by pharaohs, most notably by Rameses II.

Pectoral of Rameses II, from around 1200 BCE

Third Intermediate Period

In this 400-year-long period, Egypt was first ruled by kings descended from Libyan immigrants and later by Nubians, who ruled as the 25th Dynasty.

Ptolemaic Period

With Alexander's death, the rule of Egypt passed to Ptolemy I Soter, who established the Greek Ptolemaic Dynasty. During this time, Egypt was under threat from Rome, and its last pharaoh, Cleopatra VII, spent her life trying to make sure that Egypt remained independent.

The Ptolemies were Greek but they portrayed themselves as traditional Egyptian pharaohs

| 750 BCE | 500 BCE | 250 BCE | 1 CE |

Late Period   **Ptolemaic Period**

Late Period

The Late Period was the time between the Third Intermediate Period and Greek rule. The Nubian pharaohs were defeated by the Assyrian Empire, which ruled Egypt before Egyptian pharaohs established the 26th Dynasty. Egypt was then invaded by the Persian Empire in 525 BCE, which began the 27th Dynasty. Four more dynasties ruled Egypt before it was conquered by Alexander the Great, king of Macedon in Greece.

After Cleopatra's death in 30 BCE, Egypt fell under the rule of a number of foreign powers and did not gain independence until 1922, when it became the Republic of Egypt.

Statue of Alexander the Great

Writing

Reading and writing were important skills in ancient Egypt. Scribes—official record-keepers—were among the few people who could read and write, and they held high positions in society. Royal scribes often advised pharaohs, helping them create laws.

Writing tools

Instead of paper, Egyptians used papyrus, which was made from a reedlike plant that grew on the banks of the Nile River. The plant's stem was cut into thin strips, which were pressed together to make sheets. Writing brushes were also made from reeds that grew on the banks of the river.

Egyptian writing on papyrus

Hole for **ink** | **Wooden palette** for holding brushes | **Reed brush**

Wooden writing palette

Hieroglyphics was a writing system in which sounds, objects, and ideas were represented by pictures called hieroglyphs. It was used on tombs and monuments, and in religious texts.

The demotic script is a simplified hieroglyphic script used c. 700 BCE–250 CE for both business documents and legal works.

Greek was introduced by the Ptolemies. It is the source of many modern alphabets.

Rosetta Stone

The Egyptians wrote in different ways, using hieroglyphs in formal situations and the demotic script for daily use. However, the ability to read these scripts was lost for nearly 1,500 years. Then, in 1799, the Rosetta Stone was found, on which the same text was written in three different scripts—hieroglyphic, demotic, and Greek. By reading the Greek script, scholars eventually translated the other two and so deciphered these ancient writing symbols.

Warfare

Wars in ancient Egypt were fought mainly for economic advantages. In Nubia their presence was sometimes met with rebellion. In the Levant, during the New Kingdom, Egypt was involved in battles with small state alliances under the leadership of Mitanni and the Hittites

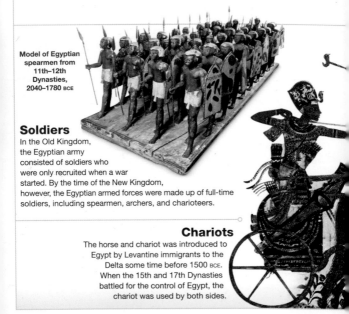

Model of Egyptian spearmen from 11th–12th Dynasties, 2040–1780 BCE

Soldiers

In the Old Kingdom, the Egyptian army consisted of soldiers who were only recruited when a war started. By the time of the New Kingdom, however, the Egyptian armed forces were made up of full-time soldiers, including spearmen, archers, and charioteers.

Chariots

The horse and chariot was introduced to Egypt by Levantine immigrants to the Delta some time before 1500 BCE. When the 15th and 17th Dynasties battled for the control of Egypt, the chariot was used by both sides.

Small-bladed ax

Long-bladed ax

Short sword

Weapons

Egyptian soldiers used axes, swords, spears, and bows and arrows. Axes and swords were used in hand-to-hand combat, while spears and bows and arrows could be used by infantry—soldiers on foot—and by charioteers.

Medals

A New Kingdom soldier could be rewarded medals in the shape of flies for bravery in combat, possibly representing the swarming army overcoming the enemy.

Tutankhamun riding a chariot into battle

The Nubians were first
hired by Egyptian armies
as temporary soldiers,
but later became an

elite
fighting
force

MEDJAY
The word "Medjay"
was first used to
refer to people living in
Medja, a part of Nubia.
After they became part
of the Egyptian armies,
the Medjay were used
as scouts for patrolling
the desert. Over time,
they became a policing
force, in charge of
protecting the royal
palace and tombs.
This model of Medjay
soldiers was found
in a tomb from the
11th–12th Dynasties.

Ancient Egyptians

Egyptian society was shaped like a pyramid. The pharaoh and his queen were at the top. Below them, the nobles, chief priests, head scribes, ministers, and army officers formed an upper class. Artisans and traders made up the middle layer, while laborers and farmers formed the base. All major decisions—in administrative and political matters, and in religious rituals—were made in the name of the pharaoh. The image on the left shows Pharaoh Tutankhamun with his queen, Ankhesenamun.

CARTOUCHE
A cartouche is an oval border around hieroglyphs that spell out a pharaoh's name. The hieroglyphs inside this cartouche spell out the name of Ramesses II.

Royal life

The Egyptians believed their pharaoh was a living god and his queen was a goddess. Nobles and important officials of the court were called "friends of the pharaoh" and lived in the palace along with the royal family. They helped the pharaoh to rule the kingdom.

Social pyramid

At the top of Egyptian society was the pharaoh. He commanded the army and ruled the country through a network of nobles, officials, and scribes. Craftworkers were kept busy building and decorating tombs and temples, but most Egyptians were peasants who worked as farmers.

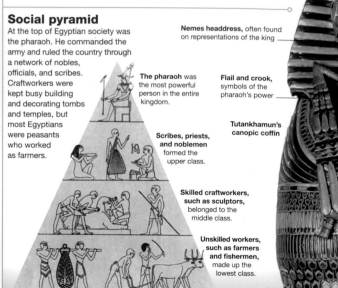

Nemes headdress, often found on representations of the king

The pharaoh was the most powerful person in the entire kingdom.

Flail and crook, symbols of the pharaoh's power

Tutankhamun's canopic coffin

Scribes, priests, and noblemen formed the upper class.

Skilled craftworkers, such as sculptors, belonged to the middle class.

Unskilled workers, such as farmers and fishermen, made up the lowest class.

Power of the pharaoh

A pharaoh had many names and titles, indicating his status and power. Two names were written within cartouches, the birth name and the throne name. Thutmose III had Thutmose ("Thoth is born") as his birth name and Menkheperre ("The manifestation of Re is established") as his throne name. Other titles included the *Nebty* name, which signified that the pharaoh was lord of both Upper and Lower Egypt. A pharaoh's regalia—his ornaments and dress—were also symbols of his power.

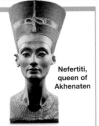

Nefertiti, queen of Akhenaten

Queens

Pharaohs had many wives, but only the one who held the title of "great royal wife" ruled beside him as his queen.

Senites, Seneb's wife

Seneb

Noblemen

Important noblemen and officials had titles like "Fanbearer on the Right of the King" and "Master of the Horse." This is a statue of Seneb, an Egyptian nobleman who held 20 titles, including "Beloved of the King."

Radjedef-Ankh, Seneb's son

FOCUS ON...
REGALIA
Each object of a pharaoh's regalia had a special significance.

Royals and nobles

Pharaohs were the supreme rulers of ancient Egypt. Their names, clothes, and regalia were all symbolic of their power. Mayors, tax collectors, and army generals helped and advised the pharaoh on political and administrative matters.

▲ The uraeus represented the goddess Wadjet as well as the divine authority of the pharaoh.

▲ The flail and crook represented the pharaoh's role as the provider and shepherd of his people.

▲ The double crown (the "Mighty One") represented the role of pharaoh as king of all of Egypt.

Djoser

Djoser is best known as the first Egyptian ruler to have a pyramid built for himself—the Step Pyramid at Saqqara. During his reign, he managed to extend the boundaries of his kingdom to the Sinai Peninsula in the east and Aswan in the south.

POSITION Pharaoh
PERIOD Old Kingdom
DYNASTY 3rd Dynasty
RULED 2667–2648 BCE

Imhotep

A leading scholar of his time, Imhotep held a number of positions under Djoser, including chief treasurer, chief scribe, and high priest of the Sun god. He designed and supervised the building of the Step Pyramid. He also wrote many books on architecture and medicine. Pictures and statues of Imhotep often show him seated with a papyrus spread across his knees.

POSITION Treasurer

PERIOD Old Kingdom

DYNASTY 3rd Dynasty

LIVED 2650–2600 BCE

After his death, Imhotep became associated with unlimited wisdom, and was worshiped as a god.

Khufu

The second pharaoh of the 4th Dynasty, Khufu came to the throne after the death of his father Sneferu. Khufu is remembered as the builder of the Great Pyramid of Giza, one of the wonders of the ancient world. The Greek historian Herodotus called him a wicked tyrant who built his pyramid using slave labor, but it is now known that the pyramid was built by craftworkers, who were well paid for their skills.

POSITION Pharaoh

PERIOD Old Kingdom

DYNASTY 4th Dynasty

RULED 2589–2566 BCE

Khafra

Khafra was the successor to Pharaoh Khufu. Egypt prospered under his reign, and there is evidence of trade with cities in other lands, such as Byblos in present-day Lebanon and Ebla in present-day Syria. This statue shows the god Horus as a falcon perched on Khafra's shoulders, protecting him.

POSITION Pharaoh
PERIOD Old Kingdom
DYNASTY 4th Dynasty
RULED 2558–2532 BCE

Userkaf

The founder of the 5th Dynasty, Userkaf began a tradition of building Sun temples at Abusir. This bust of Userkaf is the earliest statue of an Old Kingdom pharaoh wearing the deshret, or red crown, of Lower Egypt.

POSITION Pharaoh
PERIOD Old Kingdom
DYNASTY 5th Dynasty
RULED 2494–2487 BCE

Nyuserra

The name Nyuserra means "possessed of Ra's power." Nyuserra built the largest Sun temple for Ra, the Sun god, in Egypt, at Abusir. This twin statue shows him as a young and an old man.

Raneferef

Raneferef was in charge of all the artists and sculptors working for pharaohs Shepseskaf and Userkaf. He used his position to build a large tomb for himself at Saqqara, which contains two life-sized statues of him.

POSITION High Priest of Ptah

PERIOD Old Kingdom

DYNASTY 5th Dynasty

LIVED 2500–2465 BCE

POSITION Pharaoh

PERIOD Old Kingdom

DYNASTY 5th Dynasty

RULED 2445–2421 BCE

Menkaura

Khafra's son Menkaura built a much smaller pyramid than his father. This may have contributed to the much later tradition that describes Menkaura as a mild ruler.

POSITION Pharaoh

PERIOD Old Kingdom

DYNASTY 4th Dynasty

RULED 2532–2503 BCE

Mentuhotep II

During the First Intermediate Period, Egypt was divided into a number of different kingdoms. Mentuhotep II, the fifth pharaoh of the 11th Dynasty, brought Egypt under one rule and became the first pharaoh of the Middle Kingdom.

POSITION Pharaoh
PERIOD Middle Kingdom
DYNASTY 11th Dynasty
RULED
2055–2004 BCE

Painted limestone statue of Mentuhotep II

Amenemhat I

Painting of Amenemhat I in his pyramid temple at Lisht

Amenemhat I was the minister to Mentuhotep IV, the last ruler of the 11th Dynasty. After the pharaoh died, Amenemhat I took the throne and began the 12th Dynasty. To make sure that his dynasty continued to rule after he died, he made his son, Senusret I, his co-ruler. This system of co-regency was followed by all of his successors.

POSITION Pharaoh
PERIOD Middle Kingdom
DYNASTY 12th Dynasty
RULED 1985–1956 BCE

Senusret I

In 1971 BCE, Senusret I was made co-regent by his father, Amenemhat I. Texts tell of the murder of Senusret's father by his personal guards. According to the story, Senusret secretly leaves his army in Libya to travel to the capital to be crowned king. Yet another text (preserved unusually on a leather roll) tells of this king's plan to build a temple at Heliopolis.

POSITION	Pharaoh
PERIOD	Middle Kingdom
DYNASTY	12th Dynasty
RULED	1971–1926 BCE

Amenemhat II

For a brief period, Amenemhat II was a co-regent with his father Senusret I. During this time, he led a gold-mining expedition to Nubia. Treasures from his reign also include objects from Mesopotamia (in present-day Iraq) and Crete, suggesting that trade was well developed at this time.

POSITION	Pharaoh
PERIOD	Middle Kingdom
DYNASTY	12th Dynasty
RULED	1929–1895 BCE

Senusret III

Known for his military expeditions, Senusret III further expanded Egyptian rule over Nubia. He built a network of forts to keep watch along the southern border. He also built a canal through the Nile cataract at Elephantine, making it easier for ships to sail up the river.

POSITION	Pharaoh
PERIOD	Middle Kingdom
DYNASTY	12th Dynasty
RULED	1870–1831 BCE

Tetisheri

The wife of the 17th Dynasty pharaoh, Senakhtenre, Queen Tetisheri held an important place at court. She was the daughter of commoners and the owner of an estate. Tetisheri is described as the mother of the mother and mother of the father of Ahmose, who began the 18th Dynasty.

Because of her strong influence on her son and grandsons, modern scholars call Tetisheri the "Mother of the New Kingdom."

POSITION Queen and Queen Mother
PERIOD Second Intermediate Period
DYNASTY 17th–18th Dynasty
LIVED 1560–1525 BCE

Hatshepsut

One of the few women to rule Egypt, Hatshepsut was first appointed as regent for her stepson Thutmose III, who was too young to rule. In 1473 BCE, she declared herself pharaoh and began a prosperous reign that lasted 15 years.

POSITION Pharaoh
PERIOD New Kingdom
DYNASTY 18th Dynasty
RULED 1473–1458 BCE

Seqenenra Taa

When Seqenenra Taa came to the throne, most of Egypt was ruled by the Hyksos, who were of Levantine origin. Seqenenra Taa began fighting the Hyksos to free Egypt from their control. He was killed in battle, but his sons, Kamose and Ahmose, continued the war, defeating the Hyksos and beginning the New Kingdom period.

POSITION Pharaoh
PERIOD Second Intermediate Period
DYNASTY 17th Dynasty
RULED 1558–1555 BCE

Senenmut

A powerful official during the reign of Hatshepsut, Senenmut took on many roles. He was the teacher of the pharaoh's children, the architect of Hatshepsut's temple, and her close adviser.

POSITION	Architect
PERIOD	New Kingdom
DYNASTY	18th Dynasty
IN OFFICE	1473–1458 BCE

Thutmose III

One of the greatest military rulers of ancient Egypt, Thutmose III conducted 17 military campaigns and conquered around 350 cities during his reign. He built a number of temples and monuments, such as the Temple of Amun at Karnak.

POSITION	Pharaoh
PERIOD	New Kingdom
DYNASTY	18th Dynasty
RULED	1479–1425 BCE

Stab wound on head of Seqenenra's mummy

URAEI

Part of a pharaoh's regalia, a uraeus was a cobra-shaped object associated with the snake-headed goddess, Wadjet. These uraei on Pharaoh Tutankhamun's throne have Sun disks on their heads. The Sun and uraeus represented the divine authority of the pharaoh.

According to Egyptian belief, the uraei protected the pharaoh by **spitting fire** at his enemies

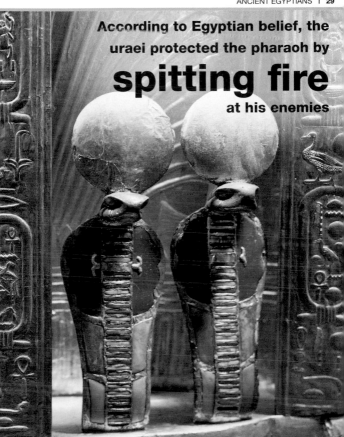

Amenhotep II

The son of Thutmose III, Amenhotep II continued his father's campaigns. He was a skilled warrior and led his armies as far as the Sea of Galilee in present-day Israel.

POSITION Pharaoh
PERIOD New Kingdom
DYNASTY 18th Dynasty
RULED 1427–1400 BCE

Sennefer

The Mayor of Thebes, Sennefer served during the reign of Amenhotep II. He was a favorite of the pharaoh, and this helped him to become very wealthy.

POSITION Mayor of Thebes
PERIOD New Kingdom
DYNASTY 18th Dynasty
IN OFFICE 1427–1400 BCE

Akhenaten

For the first five years of his reign, Akhenaten was known as Amenhotep IV. He changed his name to Akhenaten, which means "living spirit of Aten," once he began worshiping the Sun god Aten. Other gods do not appear to have been worshiped, and the name of the Theban god Amun was erased from many monuments. He also began construction of a new capital city called Akhetaten at Amarna, an area that was not associated with any of the old gods. However, the city was abandoned soon after his death.

POSITION Pharaoh
PERIOD New Kingdom
DYNASTY 18th Dynasty
RULED 1352–1336 BCE

Nefertiti

Believed to have ruled Egypt along with her husband Akhenaten, Nefertiti is now known to have lived to the end of his reign. No one knows what then happened to her, but this bust, found at Akhetaten, gives an idea of the beauty for which she was famous. In fact, her name Nefertiti means "a beautiful woman has come."

Flat-topped crown decorated with ribbon

Instead of goddesses, Akhenaten had images of Nefertiti sculpted at the four corners of his sarcophagus.

POSITION	Great Royal Wife
PERIOD	New Kingdom
DYNASTY	18th Dynasty
LIVED	1370–1338 BCE

Tutankhamun

In his short nine-year reign, Tutankhamun ended Akhenaten's ban on worshiping gods other than Aten. He also moved the royal residence back from Akhetaten to Memphis.

POSITION
Pharaoh
PERIOD
New Kingdom
DYNASTY
18th Dynasty
RULED
1336–1327 BCE

Maya

Maya held the important position of overseer of the treasury. It was his job to collect the taxes from the different parts of the kingdom.

POSITION Overseer
of the treasury
PERIOD New Kingdom
DYNASTY 18th Dynasty
LIVED 1336–1295 BCE

Maya's
wife Merit

Ramesses II

The third pharaoh of the 19th dynasty, Ramesses II was one of the greatest and most celebrated rulers of ancient Egypt. He fought the Hittites at Kadesh in 1274 BCE, and when there was no clear winner in the battle, he signed the world's earliest surviving peace treaty. A copy of this now hangs in New York City at the headquarters of the United Nations, the modern organization that deals with disputes between countries. Ramesses II ruled for more than 60 years, during which he built many monuments, such as the temples at Abu Simbel, to celebrate his achievements.

POSITION Pharaoh
PERIOD New Kingdom
DYNASTY 19th Dynasty
RULED 1279–1213 BCE

Maya

Nefertari

The chief wife of Ramesses II, Nefertari was from a noble family and married Ramesses II before he became the pharaoh. He built and dedicated the smaller temple at Abu Simbel to her. No other Egyptian queen was ever honored in this way.

POSITION	Great Royal Wife
PERIOD	New Kingdom
DYNASTY	19th Dynasty
LIVED	1279–1213 BCE

Psusennes I

The third king of the 21st Dynasty, Psusennes I was one of the few Egyptian pharaohs whose tomb was discovered intact. His burial mask, shown below, is made of gold and lapis lazuli, with black and white glass pieces for the eyes.

Eyebrows made of inlaid lapis lazuli

POSITION	Pharaoh
PERIOD	Third Intermediate Period
DYNASTY	21st Dynasty
RULED	1039–991 BCE

Sheshonq II

This stunning gold funerary mask was found covering Sheshonq II's mummy, when archaeologists found it, along with all of his grave goods, in the tomb of Psusennes I. Experts think he was buried here because his own tomb became waterlogged.

POSITION	Pharaoh
PERIOD	Third Intermediate Period
DYNASTY	22nd Dynasty
RULED	887–885 BCE

Amasis

Also known as Ahmose II, Amasis was a general in the army of Apries, the fourth pharaoh of the 26th Dynasty. In 570 BCE, Apries launched an attack against Cyrene (in present-day Libya), but failed. The Egyptian soldiers believed that Apries had betrayed them and revolted. They chose Amasis as their new pharaoh and he established a long, prosperous reign.

POSITION	Pharaoh
PERIOD	Late Period
DYNASTY	26th Dynasty
RULED	570–526 BCE

Darius I the Great

Before he became the ruler of the Persian Empire, Darius I was a soldier in the Persian army led by Emperor Cambyses. After Cambyses invaded and conquered Egypt, Darius I overthrew him and became the pharaoh.

POSITION	Pharaoh
PERIOD	Late Period
DYNASTY	27th Dynasty
RULED	522–486 BCE

Statue of Amasis as a Sphinx

Alexander the Great

One of the greatest military leaders in history, Alexander the Great was a Greek prince from Macedon. At the age of 21, he began his conquest of the known world. He defeated the Persian Empire and in 332 BCE, he came to Egypt, where he was made the pharaoh.

POSITION	Pharaoh
PERIOD	Ptolemaic Period
DYNASTY	Argead Dynasty
RULED	332–323 BCE

Ptolemy I

Founder of the Ptolemaic Dynasty, this Macedonian general succeeded Alexander the Great. Ptolemy I was a clever politician and his strategies helped him maintain peace after Alexander's death.

POSITION Pharaoh
PERIOD Ptolemaic Period
DYNASTY Ptolemaic Dynasty
RULED 305–285 BCE

Ptolemy II

The successor to Ptolemy I, Ptolemy II was co-regent until he became the ruler in 285 BCE. He was married to Arsinoe I, but banished her after becoming pharaoh. He then married his sister, a custom common in ancient Egypt, but shocking to the Greeks.

POSITION Pharaoh
PERIOD
Ptolemaic Period
DYNASTY
Ptolemaic Dynasty
RULED 285–246 BCE

Brooch showing
Ptolemy II with Arsinoe II

Arsinoe II

The sister of Ptolemy II, Arsinoe II was married to Lysimachus, the king of Thrace (in present-day Europe), but was forced to run away after his death. She came to Egypt, where she married her brother and became co-ruler. This brooch shows her with Ptolemy II.

POSITION Queen
PERIOD Ptolemaic Period
DYNASTY Ptolemaic Dynasty
LIVED 316–270 BCE

Ptolemy III

Ptolemy III married a princess of Cyrene and united the kingdoms, establishing a peaceful reign. To keep the peace, he also arranged for his sister Berenice to marry Antiochus, the king of Syria. But after Antiochus's first wife Laodice murdered Antiochus and Berenice, Ptolemy III invaded Syria to avenge his sister's death.

POSITION Pharaoh
PERIOD Ptolemaic Period
DYNASTY Ptolemaic Dynasty
RULED 246–221 BCE

Berenice II

A princess of Cyrene, Berenice II was the wife of Ptolemy III. According to legend, when Ptolemy III went to avenge the murder of his sister—also named Berenice—she cut off her hair and offered it to the gods for his safe return. The gods took her hair and turned it into a constellation called Coma Berenices.

POSITION Queen

PERIOD Ptolemaic Period

DYNASTY
Ptolemaic Dynasty

LIVED 269–221 BCE

Arsinoe III

Arsinoe III's husband, Ptolemy IV, was a weak ruler, who was controlled by his corrupt ministers. She disapproved of this corruption, but was powerless to prevent it. After her husband's death, the ministers were afraid that she would punish them, so they murdered her.

POSITION Queen

PERIOD
Ptolemaic Period

DYNASTY
Ptolemaic Dynasty

LIVED 246–204 BCE

Cleopatra VII

One of the few women to rule Egypt on her own, Cleopatra VII took many steps to prevent Rome from taking over her kingdom. She set up trade routes as far as India to keep Egypt's economy strong. She also began a romantic relationship with the Roman general Julius Caesar and, after Caesar's death, with Mark Antony. But when she and Antony were defeated by his rival Octavian, she killed herself, and Egypt became Roman territory.

POSITION Pharaoh

PERIOD Ptolemaic Period

DYNASTY
Ptolemaic Dynasty

RULED 51–30 BCE

Cleopatra VII was the last ruler of Egypt to be called Pharaoh, and was the only Ptolemaic pharaoh to speak Egyptian.

RAMESSES II

Crowned in his teens, Ramesses II ruled for around 60 years. He undertook a vast building program, expanding older temples and building new ones. During his reign, the Nile floods led to good harvests, helping him to maintain a stable kingdom. He is shown here at the annual harvest.

Ramesses II built a temple called the

Ramesseum

where only he, and no god,

was worshiped

Tombs and monuments

For the ancient Egyptians, death was only the beginning of a new life in the underworld. They built massive tombs for their dead, which were filled with treasures and objects to be used in the afterlife. The most well-known tombs are the pyramids—huge structures built for the earliest pharaohs. In the New Kingdom, tombs were dug in the Valley of the Kings near Thebes, and it is here that the greatest treasures of ancient Egypt have been found.

CANOPIC CHEST
The canopic chest of Tutankhamun contains four jars, with lids carved in his likeness. These jars contained his mummified internal organs.

Building a pyramid

During the Old Kingdom, pharaohs built huge tombs, called pyramids. Pyramids were constructed on the western bank of the Nile River, because it was thought that the land of the dead lay to the west. A single pyramid could take up to 20 years, and around 20,000 workers, to build.

Evolution of pyramids

Early tombs were single-story buildings called mastabas. The Old Kingdom architect Imhotep designed a building made of six mastabas placed one on top of the other—the first pyramid. Later, builders began filling in the pyramid sides to create the first "true pyramids."

Gilded wooden cubit rod

Boning rods

A mastaba was made of mud bricks. Inside, a deep chamber was dug, in which the dead were buried.

The Step Pyramid was designed as a stack of mastabas. It was made of small stone blocks laid like bricks.

The Great Pyramid of Giza is the world's largest true pyramid. It was built by placing large stone blocks together, which were then overlaid with polished limestone.

Building tools

The sides of true pyramids were angled at 52-53 degrees, and all the stones were cut to the same size. Egyptian builders used tools such as the triangle to measure the angles, cubit rods to measure lengths, and boning rods to make sure that the stones were even.

Triangle

Pyramid builders

Laborers carried stones from quarries, sometimes over long distances, to build pyramids. At the construction site they would lift the stones using ropes, or drag them up a ramp and lay them using cement or mortar.

Pyramids

The pyramids of Egypt have fascinated people for thousands of years. These massive stone structures were built as the final resting places for pharaohs and members of their families. There are more than 100 pyramids spread across Egypt.

FOCUS ON...
BUILDING MATERIALS
The Egyptians used many different types of stone to build pyramids

---

Great Pyramid of Giza

The largest pyramid ever built, the Great Pyramid of Giza took 20 years and about 2,300,000 blocks of limestone to complete. Each block weighs an average of 2.75 tons (2.5 metric tonnes). Inside, the pyramid has a huge network of passages, galleries, and hidden chambers, some of which have not been explored even to this day.

DEDICATED TO Khufu

BUILT IN 2589 BCE
(4th Dynasty Old Kingdom)

SIZE 482 ft (147 m) tall

LOCATION Giza

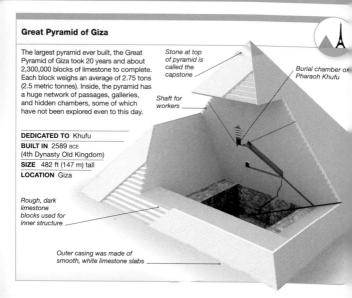

Stone at top of pyramid is called the capstone

Burial chamber of Pharaoh Khufu

Shaft for workers

Rough, dark limestone blocks used for inner structure

Outer casing was made of smooth, white limestone slabs

In the Old Kingdom, pyramids were made of limestone blocks. Sketches and plans of pyramids were also drawn on pieces of limestone.

The statues, tablets, and sarcophagi that were placed inside the pyramids, were made of black basalt.

Pyramids in the Middle Kingdom were made mostly of mud bricks. Limestone was used as an outer casing.

Pyramid of Khafra

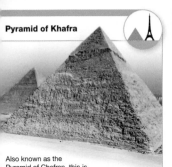

Also known as the Pyramid of Chefren, this is the second largest of the pyramids of Giza. Pharaoh Khafra built this pyramid on higher ground, so that it would look like his pyramid was taller than Khufu's.

DEDICATED TO Khafra

BUILT IN 2520 BCE (4th Dynasty Old Kingdom)

SIZE 472 ft (144 m) tall

LOCATION Giza

Pyramid of Menkaura

The last pyramid to be built at Giza, the Pyramid of Menkaura is much smaller than its neighbors. At its southern foot, three smaller pyramids were built for the wives of Pharaoh Menkaura.

DEDICATED TO Menkaura

BUILT IN 2490 BCE (4th Dynasty Old Kingdom)

SIZE 213 ft (65 m) tall

LOCATION Giza

Pyramid of Menkaura's queen

Pyramid of Neferirkara

While the pyramid was being built, its intended user—Pharaoh Neferirkara—died, and so it was left unfinished. It was designed to be a step pyramid with six levels, but during its construction, the builders decided to fill in the steps to give it the shape of a true pyramid.

DEDICATED TO Neferirkara

BUILT IN 2475–2455 BCE (5th Dynasty Old Kingdom)

SIZE 230 ft (70 m) tall

LOCATION Abusir

Pyramid of Sahura

Pyramid of Teti

Although its outer casing has broken down over the years, making it look like a pile of rubble, the Pyramid of Teti has well-preserved chambers and corridors inside. The walls of the burial chamber are inscribed with texts and the chamber ceiling is painted with stars.

DEDICATED TO Teti

BUILT IN 2323–2291 BCE (6th Dynasty Old Kingdom)

SIZE 170 ft (52.5 m) tall

LOCATION Saqqara

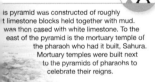

...is pyramid was constructed of roughly ...t limestone blocks held together with mud. ...was then cased with white limestone. To the east of the pyramid is the mortuary temple of the pharaoh who had it built, Sahura. Mortuary temples were built next to the pyramids to celebrate their reigns.

Ruins of Sahura's mortuary temple

DEDICATED TO Sahura

BUILT IN 2487–2475 BCE (5th Dynasty Old kingdom)

SIZE 154 ft (47 m) tall

LOCATION Abusir

Bent Pyramid

Also known as the Gleaming Pyramid of the South, the Bent Pyramid was originally designed to have a steep angle of 54 degrees. But this made the structure unstable. The builders then changed the angle of the remaining part to 43 degrees, giving the pyramid its unique shape.

DEDICATED TO Sneferu

BUILT IN 2613–2589 BCE
(4th Dynasty Old Kingdom)

SIZE 330 ft (100 m) tall

LOCATION Dashur

Red Pyramid

Pharaoh Sneferu tried three times to build a true pyramid. His first two attempts—the Meidum Pyramid and the Bent Pyramid—failed. It was only with the Red Pyramid that he succeeded. This pyramid gets its name from the red sandstone found at its base.

DEDICATED TO Sneferu

BUILT IN 2613–2589 BCE
(4th Dynasty Old Kingdom)

SIZE 345 ft (105 m) tall

LOCATION Dashur

Meidum Pyramid

The construction of the Meidum Pyramid was started by an earlier ruler but completed by Pharaoh Sneferu. It was first built as a step pyramid with eight steps. These steps were later filled in and an outer casing was added. Over the centuries, the outer casing has collapsed and only the central core now remains.

DEDICATED TO	Sneferu
BUILT IN	2613–2589 BCE (4th Dynasty Old Kingdom)
SIZE	213 ft (65 m) tall
LOCATION	Fayum

Most of the limestone casing of this pyramid was removed and used to build the city of Cairo.

Pyramid of Unas

From the outside, this looks more like a small hill or rubble than a royal pyramid. What makes it so important is the presence of the earliest Egyptian religious texts, called pyramid texts, covering the walls of the burial chamber. They are a collection of spells meant to protect the dead in the afterlife.

DEDICATED TO Unas

BUILT IN 2375–2345 BCE
(5th Dynasty Old Kingdom)

SIZE 62 ft (18.5 m) tall

LOCATION Saqqara

Step Pyramid

Pyramid of Userkaf

The mortuary temple of this pyramid complex faces south instead of east, which was usually the case. This was probably done because Userkaf worshiped the Sun, and this way, the temple would remain in sunlight all day long.

DEDICATED TO Userkaf

BUILT IN 2494–2487 BCE
(5th Dynasty Old Kingdom)

SIZE 160 ft (49 m) tall

LOCATION Abusir

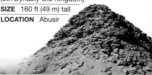

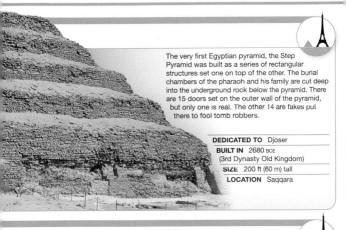

The very first Egyptian pyramid, the Step Pyramid was built as a series of rectangular structures set one on top of the other. The burial chambers of the pharaoh and his family are cut deep into the underground rock below the pyramid. There are 15 doors set on the outer wall of the pyramid, but only one is real. The other 14 are fakes put there to fool tomb robbers.

DEDICATED TO Djoser

BUILT IN 2680 BCE
(3rd Dynasty Old Kingdom)

SIZE 200 ft (60 m) tall

LOCATION Saqqara

Black Pyramid

Also known as the Pyramid of Amenemhat III, the Black Pyramid was an architectural disaster. It was built on unstable ground very near to the Nile River. This allowed water to seep in and weaken the structure. Although the damage was repaired, the pharaoh chose not to use it and had another tomb built for himself at Hawara.

DEDICATED TO Amenemhat III

BUILT IN 1860–1814 BCE
(12th Dynasty Middle Kingdom)

SIZE 246 ft (75 m) tall

LOCATION Dashur

The entire outer casing of the
Meidum Pyramid has crumbled
away, giving it the nickname

"the collapsed pyramid"

BREAKING DOWN
There are several
theories about the
collapse of the Meidum
Pyramid. Some people
believe its shape put a
lot of pressure on the
structure. Others argue
that an earthquake
weakened the building.

Tombs

Instead of pyramids, pharaohs of the New Kingdom chose underground tombs cut deep into mountains as their burial sites in order to foil robbers. The largest site of such tombs is the Valley of the Kings near Thebes. By 2012, 63 tombs had been discovered here. Next to this site is the Valley of the Queens, where more than 70 tombs of queens and princesses have been found.

Tomb of Ramesses VII

Because of its location at the entrance of the Valley of the Kings, this tomb was given the name KV 1. It has only one burial chamber, with a small hollow beyond it, which is believed to be an unfinished room. A painting on the right wall shows the gods reviving the Sun disk in fire.

TOMB NUMBER KV 1

BUILT IN 1136–1129 BCE
(20th Dynasty New Kingdom)

LOCATION Valley of the Kings, Thebes

Tomb of Ramesses IV

Ancient Greek and Roman travelers often used the tombs in the Valley as shelters. KV 2 was one such tomb. It contains drawings and inscriptions by different travelers who stayed in the tomb. Visitors inscribed their name, profession, place of origin, and personal comments about the tomb.

TOMB NUMBER KV 2

BUILT IN 1155–1149 BCE (20th Dynasty New Kingdom)

LOCATION Valley of the Kings, Thebes

Tomb of the sons of Ramesses II

This tomb was considered an unimportant hole in the ground until the remains of the sons of Ramesses II were discovered by a team of archeologists in 1995. It is the largest tomb in the Valley. Up to 121 chambers and corridors have been found so far and experts believe that the tomb may have 150 chambers in total.

Statue of Osiris is found in corridor number seven

TOMB NUMBER KV 5

BUILT IN 1279–1213 BCE (19th Dynasty New Kingdom)

LOCATION Valley of the Kings, Thebes

Tomb of Ramesses V and Ramesses VI

Ramesses V began building this tomb for himself, but it was completed by his brother and successor, Ramesses VI, who decorated the new sections with his own name and images. However, since no mummies have been found inside the tomb, it is not known if Ramesses VI was the only pharaoh to be buried in it, or if the two pharaohs were buried next to each other.

TOMB NUMBER KV 9

BUILT IN 1149–1137 BCE (20th Dynasty New Kingdom)

LOCATION Valley of the Kings, Thebes

Tomb of Amenhotep III

One of the oldest tombs in the Valley, KV 22 has been completely looted and every trace of gold or precious metal has been removed. The lid of the sarcophagus was broken into several pieces, but has now been restored.

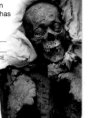

TOMB NUMBER KV 22

BUILT IN 1390–1352 BCE (18th Dynasty New Kingdom)

LOCATION Valley of the Kings, Thebes

Tomb of Tutankhamun

The entrance to KV 62 was hidden under a pile of rock and debris during the construction of KV 9, keeping it safe from tomb robbers. This is why it was found almost completely intact and still containing most of its treasures.

Tomb of Amenhotep II

This tomb is located in the southwestern part of the Valley of the Kings. It shows signs of having been looted repeatedly, but luckily, the mummy of Amenhotep II was found intact inside its sarcophagus. The tomb was also used to store other royal mummies, including those of Thutmose IV, Amenhotep III, Seti II, and Ramesses IV.

Sarcophagus of Amenhotep II

TOMB NUMBER	KV 35
BUILT IN	1425–1400 BCE (18th Dynasty New Kingdom)
LOCATION	Valley of the Kings, Thebes

TOMB NUMBER	KV 62
BUILT IN	1333–1323 BCE (18th Dynasty New Kingdom)
LOCATION	Valley of Kings, Thebes

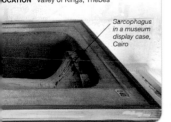

Sarcophagus in a museum display case, Cairo

Tomb of Seti I

This is the longest and deepest tomb in the Valley. Its walls are covered with religious paintings in which the pharaoh is shown with different deities. This painting shows Nephthys, protector of the dead, holding him in her arms.

TOMB NUMBER	KV 17
BUILT IN	1290–1279 BCE (19th Dynasty New Kingdom)
LOCATION	Valley of the Kings, Thebes

Tomb of Ay

Also called Southern Tomb 25, this is one of 25 tombs discovered near Akhetaten. It contains paintings of Ay, an Egyptian nobleman, and his family praying to the Sun god Aten. It has, painted on its walls, one of the longest hymns to Aten ever found.

TOMB NUMBER Amarna Tomb 25

BUILT IN 1352–1334 BCE
(18th Dynasty New Kingdom)

LOCATION Amarna

Tomb of Sennefer

Tombs of royal courtiers and nobles were built near the Valley of the Kings. This is the tomb of Sennefer, the mayor of Thebes. It is entered through a steep tunnel, which leads to a set of chambers. The ceiling of the tomb is decorated with grape vines, which has given the tomb its nickname of "tomb of vines."

TOMB NUMBER TT 96

BUILT IN 1425–1400 BCE
(18th Dynasty New Kingdom)

LOCATION Tombs of the Nobles, Thebes

Tomb of Menna

This tomb was built for Menna, a scribe and supervisor of the lands belonging to the pharaoh. The paintings inside the tomb show scenes from Menna's life. In this image, he can be seen sitting in front of a table laden with food. Other paintings show him supervising farmers and recording the harvest.

TOMB NUMBER TT 69

BUILT IN 1400–1352 BCE
(18th Dynasty New Kingdom)

LOCATION Sheikh Abd el-Qurna, Thebes

Tomb of Peshedu

The builders and artists who worked on royal tombs lived in a village near the Valley of the Kings, now called Deir el-Medina, or "workers' village." The site also contains the tombs of these craftworkers. TT 3 was built for Peshedu, who was an overseer of tomb artists. Its walls and ceiling are decorated with paintings of deities and religious symbols.

TOMB NUMBER	TT 3
BUILT IN	1149–1137 BCE (20th Dynasty New Kingdom)
LOCATION	Deir el-Medina, Thebes

The god Ptah shown in the form of a falcon   *Wadjet eye*

Tomb of Nefertari

Built by Ramesses II for his wife Nefertari, QV 66 contains paintings of the queen being presented to the gods, as well as texts from the Book of the Dead, believed to aid her journey into immortality.

TOMB NUMBER
QV 66

BUILT IN
1279–1213 BCE
(19th Dynasty
New Kingdom)

LOCATION Valley
of the Queens,
Thebes

The paintings on the walls
of Nefertari's tomb show the
journey of
her soul
to the afterlife

NEFERTARI'S TOMB
Discovered in 1904, QV 66, the tomb of Nefertari, is famous for its beautiful paintings, which depict the queen being presented before the main gods of ancient Egypt. She is shown here with Khepri, the scarab god, Horus, the falcon god, and Osiris, ruler of the underworld.

Tomb treasures

Pyramids and other tombs contained many artifacts and treasures.
These were meant to help the dead live comfortably in the afterlife.
However, most tombs were robbed and their priceless contents
stolen in ancient times. The tomb of Pharaoh Tutankhaum was
discovered almost intact and filled with glittering treasures.

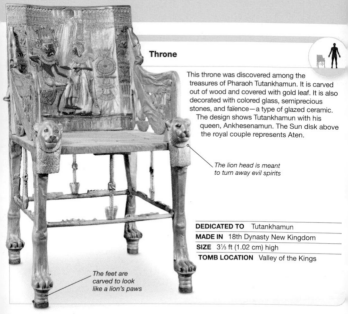

Throne

This throne was discovered among the
treasures of Pharaoh Tutankhamun. It is carved
out of wood and covered with gold leaf. It is also
decorated with colored glass, semiprecious
stones, and faïence—a type of glazed ceramic.
The design shows Tutankhamun with his
queen, Ankhesenamun. The Sun disk above
the royal couple represents Aten.

*The lion head is meant
to turn away evil spirits*

DEDICATED TO	Tutankhamun
MADE IN	18th Dynasty New Kingdom
SIZE	3⅓ ft (1.02 cm) high
TOMB LOCATION	Valley of the Kings

*The feet are
carved to look
like a lion's paws*

Sarcophagus

When the tomb of Thutmose III was discovered in 1898, all that remained was some broken furniture, as well as statues and this sarcophagus. Everything else had been taken by tomb robbers. The sarcophagus is decorated with carvings of Egyptian gods and goddesses, and hieroglyphs.

DEDICATED TO Thutmose III

MADE IN 18th Dynasty New Kingdom

SIZE 7½ ft (2.35 m) long

TOMB LOCATION Valley of the Kings

Solar boat

In 1950, archeologists discovered a ship at the base of the Great Pyramid of Giza. One of the world's oldest boats, it was built for Pharaoh Khufu and buried as part of his funeral treasure. Also known as a solar boat, the ship was meant to help Khufu travel to the underworld.

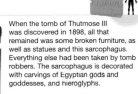

The entire ship was built and then separated into 1,224 pieces, which were buried under thick limestone slabs.

DEDICATED TO Khufu

MADE IN 4th Dynasty Old Kingdom

SIZE 143 ft (43.6 m) long

TOMB LOCATION Giza

Hapi canopic jar

Canopic jars were used to store a mummy's organs. They were made to resemble one of the four sons of the god Horus, representing north, south, east, and west. This jar has the baboon-shaped head of Hapi, who stood for the north. It was placed facing north and contained the lungs.

DEDICATED TO Unknown

MADE IN 25th Dynasty Third Intermediate Period

SIZE 11 in (28 cm) tall

TOMB LOCATION Unknown

Qebehsenuef canopic jar

Qebehsenuef, the falcon-headed son of Horus, represented the west, and protected the intestines of the mummy. This jar was made for the mummy of Paiduf, a priest of the god Amun.

DEDICATED TO Paiduf

MADE IN 22nd Dynasty Third Intermediate Period

SIZE 11¾ in (29.5 cm) tall

TOMB LOCATION Unknown

Canopic shrine

The word "canopic" comes from the town of Canopus, where Osiris was worshiped in the form of a vase with a human head.

Canopic jars were placed inside a chest, which was then put inside a shrine. This canopic shrine was found in the tomb of Tutankhamun. It has a statue of a different goddess on each side. The goddess seen here is Serqet, the scorpion goddess.

DEDICATED TO Tutankhamun

MADE IN 18th Dynasty New Kingdom

SIZE 6½ ft (2 m)

TOMB LOCATION Valley of the Kings, Thebes

Duamutef canopic jar

Jackal-headed Duamutef stood for the east and protected the stomach in the afterlife. The jar was placed with the head facing east.

DEDICATED TO Paiduf

MADE IN 22nd Dynasty Third Intermediate Period

SIZE 11¾ in (29.5 cm) tall

TOMB LOCATION Unknown

Imseti canopic jar

The only son of Horus and with the face of a human, Imseti was the protector of the liver. He represented the south and so the jar was placed with his head facing that direction.

DEDICATED TO Unknown

MADE IN 25th Dynasty Third Intermediate Period

SIZE 12 in (31 cm) tall

TOMB LOCATION Unknown

Headrest

The Egyptians used headrests rather than pillows. This ivory headrest has been carved in the shape of Shu, the god of air. He is shown separating Earth from the sky. The lions on each side represent the eastern and western horizons.

DEDICATED TO
Tutankhamun

MADE IN 18th Dynasty
New Kingdom

SIZE 6¾ in (17.5 cm) long

TOMB LOCATION Valley of the Kings, Thebes

Earring

Earrings became common in Egypt during the New Kingdom. These earrings, made of gold and colored glass, were buried with Pharaoh Tutankhamun in his tomb.

DEDICATED TO Tutankhamun

MADE IN 18th Dynasty
New Kingdom

SIZE 3–4 in (8–10 cm) long

TOMB LOCATION Valley of the Kings, Thebes

Pendant

Designed in the shape of a winged scarab beetle holding the disk of the Sun, this pendant also spells out "Nebkheperure," which was the throne name of Tutankhamun. The basket shape at the bottom spells "neb," the beetle spells "kheperu," and the Sun disk spells out "re."

DEDICATED TO Tutankhamun

MADE IN 18th Dynasty
New Kingdom

SIZE 3½ in (9 cm) tall

TOMB LOCATION Valley of the Kings, Thebes

Mirror case

This mirror case is designed in the shape of an ankh, a hieroglyph that means "eternal life." The scarab decoration spells out Tutankhamun's name. There used to be a mirror inside the case, but it was stolen in ancient times.

DEDICATED TO Tutankhamun

MADE IN 18th Dynasty New Kingdom

SIZE 10½ in (27 cm) tall

TOMB LOCATION Valley of the Kings, Thebes

Pectoral

Found inside one of Tutankhamun's treasure boxes, this pectoral (jewelry worn on the chest) shows the pharaoh with the goddess Ma'at. He is wearing a war helmet and receiving an ankh from the goddess.

DEDICATED TO Tutankhamun

MADE IN 18th Dynasty New Kingdom

SIZE 3½ in (9 cm) wide

TOMB LOCATION Valley of the Kings, Thebes

Gilt shrine

This tiny wooden shrine is covered with embossed sheets of gold, which show Queen Ankhesenamun with Tutankhamun. The shrine once contained a statue, but it was stolen by tomb robbers in ancient times.

DEDICATED TO Tutankhamun

MADE IN 18th Dynasty New Kingdom

SIZE 20¼ in (50.5 cm) tall

TOMB LOCATION Valley of the Kings, Thebes

Monuments

In addition to pyramids and tombs, the Egyptians also built monuments to honor their rulers and gods. They used limestone and granite for building, since these materials were readily available. From these, Egyptian artists created giant sculptures, such as the Great Sphinx and the Colossi of Memnon, which have lasted for centuries.

Great Sphinx

For more than 4,500 years, the Sphinx has guarded Khafre's pyramid at Giza. Carved from a huge outcrop of limestone, it is the largest free-standing sculpture to survive from ancient times. It has the body of a lion and the head of a pharaoh.

DEDICATED TO Khafre

BUILT IN 2558–2532 BCE (4th Dynasty Old Kingdom)

SIZE 66 ft (20 m) tall

LOCATION Giza

Limestone eroded by wind, sand, and pollution

Alabaster sphinx of Memphis

Although smaller than the Great Sphinx in Giza, the alabaster sphinx of Memphis is an impressive example of Egyptian art. It is made of the mineral calcite and weighs about 88 tons (80 metric tonnes), making it the largest calcite statue ever found.

DEDICATED TO Hatshepsut

BUILT IN 1473–1458 BCE
(18th Dynasty New Kingdom)

SIZE 26 ft (8 m) tall

LOCATION Memphis

Colossi of Memnon

On the western bank of the Nile River stand the two Colossi of Memnon. These giants were originally built to guard the temple of Amenhotep III, which was looted by later pharaohs and eventually destroyed by floods. The statues show Amenhotep III seated, with his hands resting on his knees, looking east toward the rising Sun.

The faces of the statues have been destroyed over time

DEDICATED TO Amenhotep III

BUILT IN 1390–1352 BCE
(18th Dynasty New Kingdom)

SIZE 59 ft (18 m) tall

LOCATION Thebes

Seated colossus of Ramesses II

This statue of Pharaoh Ramesses II stands inside the Luxor Temple. It is made of granite and was built to celebrate the pharaoh's victory over the Hittites in the Battle of Kadesh in 1274 BCE.

DEDICATED TO Ramesses II

BUILT IN 1279–1213 BCE (19th Dynasty New Kingdom)

SIZE 26 ft (8 m) tall

LOCATION Luxor Temple

Baboon statue

Baboons were the sacred animals of Thoth, the god of wisdom. This baboon statue was erected by Amenhotep III. It is one of four baboon statues placed by the pharaoh at the Temple of Thoth in Hermopolis.

DEDICATED TO Thoth

BUILT IN 1390–1352 BCE (18th Dynasty New Kingdom)

SIZE 14¾ ft (4.5 m) tall

LOCATION Hermopolis

Criosphinx

Pyramidion

The top stone of a pyramid was called a pyramidion. The tombs from the workers' village Deir el-Medina included chapels crowned with steep-sided pyramids. The pyramidions from these tombs were decorated with images of their owners worshiping the Sun god. This one has a hieroglyphic prayer to the Sun god Ra.

DEDICATED TO Ra

BUILT IN 19th Dynasty New Kingdom

SIZE 16 in (40 cm) tall

LOCATION Deir el-Medina

Cleopatra's Needle

Thutmose III constructed this 265-ton (240-metric-tonne) granite obelisk at Heliopolis. Nearly 200 years later, Ramesses II added the inscriptions to mark his military victories. In 1877, the Egyptian government gave the obelisk to the US as a gift, where it was nicknamed Cleopatra's Needle. Two other obelisks—in London and Paris, are also called this.

DEDICATED TO Horus

BUILT IN 1450 BCE (18th Dynasty Middle Kingdom)

SIZE 69 ft (21 m)

LOCATION Originally in Heliopolis; transported to New York City in 1877

The southern entrance to the Karnak Temple is an avenue that is lined with a row of structures called Criosphinxes. These have the body of a lion and the head of a ram. The figure between the paws of this criosphinx is that of a pharaoh, believed to be Amenhotep III.

DEDICATED TO Amun

BUILT IN Middle Kingdom to Ptolemaic Period

SIZE 4 ft (1.2 m) tall

LOCATION Karnak Temple

Although the obelisk is now called Cleopatra's Needle, it was built more than 1,000 years before Cleopatra's birth.

According to legend, Thutmose IV dreamed that the Sphinx promised to make him

ruler of all Egypt

if he cleared away the sand covering it

GREAT SPHINX
The Great Sphinx is thought to be a form of the god Horus—protector of the pharaoh. When Thutmose IV came to the throne, he had a tablet, called the dream stela, built. This tablet, located between the paws of the Sphinx, tells the story of how the Sphinx made Thutmose IV the ruler of Egypt.

Religion

The Egyptians worshiped hundreds of gods and goddesses. Many deities were represented by animals, but the most powerful ones were always represented by the disk of the Sun. Temples were called the homes of the gods, and the priests who lived in them were known as the gods' servants. Here, the ram-headed god Khnum and the goddesses Hathor and Ma'at are wearing Sun disks on their heads.

KNOT OF ISIS
Amulets were worn to ward off evil. This knot-shaped amulet was associated with the goddess Isis and was placed on mummies to protect them in the afterlife.

Mythology

Ancient Egyptians worshiped hundreds of deities (gods and goddesses)—an ancient text lists as many as 740. Some were local, while others were worshiped throughout the kingdom. All the forces of nature, including the wind, rain, and Sun, were represented by deitie

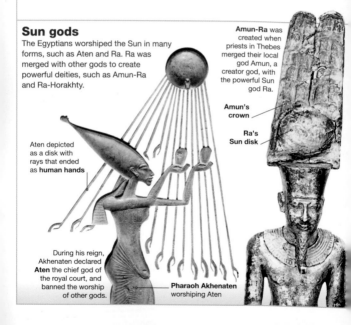

Sun gods

The Egyptians worshiped the Sun in many forms, such as Aten and Ra. Ra was merged with other gods to create powerful deities, such as Amun-Ra and Ra-Horakhty.

Amun-Ra was created when priests in Thebes merged their local god Amun, a creator god, with the powerful Sun god Ra.

Amun's crown

Ra's Sun disk

Aten depicted as a disk with rays that ended as **human hands**

During his reign, Akhenaten declared **Aten** the chief god of the royal court, and banned the worship of other gods.

Pharaoh Akhenaten worshiping Aten

Groups of gods

Different groups of deities were worshiped in different cities. In Memphis, the triad (group of three, shown on the right) of Ptah, Sekhmet, and Nefertum was worshiped. In Heliopolis, the main deities were a group of nine, called the Ennead, shown below. The arrows show how some gods were the parents of others.

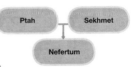

Memphis Triad

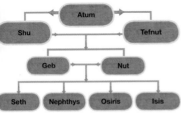

Ennead of Heliopolis

Ra-Horakhty was a falcon-headed Sun god and a version of the sky god Horus. He was the protector of the pharaohs.

— **Sun disk** of Ra

— **Falcon head** of Horus

Pharaoh as god

Egyptians believed that after a pharaoh died, he became a god. He was often shown in statues and paintings with other gods. Dead pharaohs were worshiped in buildings called mortuary temples.

Priests and rituals

Ancient Egyptians were deeply religious and believed that everything in their lives was controlled by gods and goddesses. In order to live a happy life and enter the afterlife, they performed rituals for the gods at important events, such as births, funerals, festivals, and royal coronations.

Role of priests

As the overseers of all religious rituals, priests led prayers and religious processions, and also made offerings to the gods. This painting shows Deniuenkhons, an Egyptian priestess, making offerings to the god Ra-Harakhty. The offerings include a plucked fowl, loaves of bread, lettuce, and a jar of beer. Priests also supervised the making of mummies, making sure that the appropriate spells were spoken and that protective amulets were placed correctly on the mummy.

Animal cults

Animal cults were an important part of Egyptian religion. The Apis Bull was a black calf with certain markings on its body, such as a diamond-shaped white patch on the forehead and a scarab-shaped mark under its tongue. It was worshiped as a form of Osiris. During religious festivals, it was dressed with colorful flowers and cloth and led through the streets by priests.

Mummification

Priests played an important part in mummification rituals. One priest would act as the jackel-headed god Anubis, who is often shown at the mummification of Osiris. Several of the masks used on these occasions have been discovered.

Mummies and the afterlife

Ka statue of Pharaoh Hor

The Egyptians believed in an afterlife where they would be reborn in their original bodies. For this to happen, the body had to be preserved in the form of a mummy. Before reaching the afterlife, the spirits of the dead were thought to journey through an underworld called *Duat*.

Forms of a soul

There were two important spirits that made up a person. The *ka*, which was the life-force, was symbolized by two raised hands. The *ba*, or soul, was symbolized by a bird with a human head.

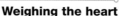

Weighing the heart

In *Duat*, spirits were judged for their sins in the Hall of Judgment. The god Anubis weighed their hearts against a feather of Ma'at, the goddess of truth. If the heart was heavier than the feather, it meant that the person had committed many sins in life and was not allowed to be reborn—the soul was fed to the goddess Ammut "the devourer" and the person died a second time, losing the possibility of eternal life.

The art of mummification

The mummification of a body was a complex process, involving numerous rituals and magic spells performed by priests. The main priest performed his duties wearing an Anubis mask, as seen below.

The body was cleaned using water and salt. The internal organs were taken out and placed in canopic jars.

The body was filled with bags of salt for 40 days, to dry it, after which it was stuffed with bandages and spices.

It was then coated with resin (a tree sap) and wrapped in linen strips over a period of 15 days, along with protective amulets.

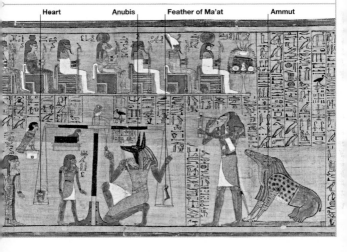

Heart · Anubis · Feather of Ma'at · Ammut

Gods and goddesses

The gods and goddesses of ancient Egypt were believed to control the movement of the Sun across the sky, the flooding of the Nile River, the afterlife, and childbirth. Each city and village had its patron god, and as the popularity of the god grew, he or she was given a higher status than other gods.

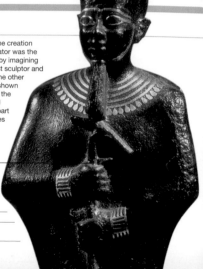

Ptah

The Egyptians had many myths about the creation of the world. In one such myth, the creator was the god Ptah. He formed all the other gods by imagining and naming them. Ptah was also the first sculptor and metalworker, using his skills to create the other beings of the universe. Ptah was often shown holding a staff that was decorated with the head of an animal. This staff was called the was scepter. He was worshiped as part of the Memphis Triad—a group of deities that included Nefertum and Sekhmet.

The was scepter symbolizes Ptah's power over chaos

RELATED SYMBOL Bull or Djed pillar

ALTERNATIVE NAMES None

PERIOD WORSHIPED Old Kingdom to Ptolemaic Period

CENTER OF WORSHIP Memphis

Nefertum

Headdress in shape of lotus flower

Ancient Egyptians believed that Nefertum was born from a blue lotus at the time of creation. He was worshiped in the Momphis Triad as the son of Ptah and Sekhmet. Amulets representing him were made in the shape of lotus flowers and were thought to bring good luck.

Nefertum was often shown with blue skin

RELATED SYMBOL Lotus

ALTERNATIVE NAMES Nefer-tum

PERIOD WORSHIPED Old Kingdom to Ptolemaic Period

CENTER OF WORSHIP Memphis

Sekhmet

The third deity in the Memphis Triad, Sekhmet was Ptah's companion. A war goddess, Sekhmet fought and destroyed the enemies of Ra. She was also associated with medicine and healing.

RELATED SYMBOL Lioness

ALTERNATIVE NAMES Sakhmet

PERIOD WORSHIPED Old Kingdom to Ptolemaic Period

CENTER OF WORSHIP Memphis

Shu

The god of air, Shu was created by the breath of Atum. Shu was part of the Ennead of Heliopolis—a group of nine gods. He and his sister-companion Tefnut were the parents of Geb, the god of Earth, and Nut, the goddess of the sky.

RELATED SYMBOL
Ostrich feather

ALTERNATIVE NAME Su

PERIOD WORSHIPED
Old Kingdom to Ptolemaic Period

CENTER OF WORSHIP
Heliopolis

Tefnut

Tefnut was the goddess of moisture and rain. In 2200 BCE, a drought spread across Egypt. People believed that this was because she had argued with Shu and left the country, taking the rain with her.

RELATED SYMBOL
Lioness

ALTERNATIVE NAMES
Tefenet, Tefnet

PERIOD WORSHIPED
Old Kingdom to Ptolemaic Period

CENTER OF WORSHIP
Heliopolis

Atum

One of the oldest gods of Egypt, Atum was the chief god of the Ennead of Heliopolis. Over time, he merged with the god Ra. This new deity was worshiped as Atum-Ra, who was considered as the creator of the other gods of the Ennead.

RELATED SYMBOL Scarab beetle

ALTERNATIVE NAMES Tem or Temu

PERIOD WORSHIPED Old Kingdom to Ptolemaic Period

CENTER OF WORSHIP Heliopolis

Geb and Nut

Geb and Nut were the gods of Earth and the sky respectively. Geb's body was Earth, and his laughter caused earthquakes. Nut's body was the sky and was covered with stars.

RELATED SYMBOLS Man lying on ground (Geb) and woman arching over him (Nut)

ALTERNATIVE NAMES Seb, Keb, or Kebb (Geb) and Nuit or Nwt (Nut)

PERIOD WORSHIPED Old Kingdom to Ptolemaic Period

CENTER OF WORSHIP Heliopolis

Nephthys

The daughter of Geb and Nut, Nephthys was the goddess of help and protection. She is the ghostly figure behind Isis in this picture. She kept the dead safe on their way to the underworld.

RELATED SYMBOL Hieroglyph showing house and basket

ALTERNATIVE NAMES Nebhet

PERIOD WORSHIPED Old Kingdom to Ptolemaic Period

CENTER OF WORSHIP Heliopolis

Isis

The goddess of family life, Isis was the wife of Osiris and the mother of Horus. After Osiris was killed by his brother Seth, she brought him back to life with a spell called the "Ritual of Life." This spell was later given to the Egyptians so that their dead could live forever in the afterlife.

RELATED SYMBOL Cow horns

ALTERNATIVE NAMES Aset, Ast, Iset, Uset

PERIOD WORSHIPED Old Kingdom to Roman Period

CENTER OF WORSHIP Philae

Anubis

Ancient Egyptians often saw jackals scavenging in cemeteries, and so the jackal-headed god Anubis became closely linked with the dead. In paintings, Anubis is often shown preparing a body for mummification, as well as performing the "opening of the mouth" ritual.

RELATED SYMBOL Jackal or wild dog

ALTERNATIVE NAMES None

PERIOD WORSHIPED Old Kingdom to Ptolemaic Period

CENTERS OF WORSHIP Lycopolis (Modern-day Asyut) and Cynopolis

Seth

Seth was the god of the desert, violence, and thunderstorms. He had the body of a man, but the face of a strange, mythical creature. Although he was the chief rival of Horus—the patron god of pharaohs—Egyptians admired Seth for his strength and ferocity. This image from the throne of Sesostris I shows both Seth and Horus. Seth represents Lower Egypt, while Horus stands for Upper Egypt.

RELATED SYMBOL Seth animal

ALTERNATIVE NAMES Set

PERIOD WORSHIPED Old Kingdom to Ptolemaic Period

CENTER OF WORSHIP Ombos (near Naqada)

Anubis's fur was not reddish brown like a jackal's, but black This was because the color black symbolized rebirth.

Osiris

According to an Egyptian myth, the god Osiris was the first ruler of Egypt. He was murdered by Seth, who wanted the kingdom for himself. After his wife Isis brought him back to life, he became a god and ruler of the underworld. Because he had been resurrected, or brought back to life, Osiris became the god of resurrection and a symbol of immortality.

RELATED SYMBOL
Crook and flail

ALTERNATIVE NAMES Asir

PERIOD WORSHIPED
Old Kingdom to Ptolemaic Period

CENTER OF WORSHIP
Abydos

Horus

A sky god, Horus was the son of Osiris and Isis. He was born after Seth murdered Osiris. Horus fought Seth for 80 years, defeating him and becoming the ruler of Egypt.

Statue of Horus in the form of a falcon

RELATED SYMBOL
Falcon or hawk

ALTERNATIVE NAMES
Heru, Hor, Har

PERIOD WORSHIPED Old Kingdom to Ptolemaic Period

CENTERS OF WORSHIP
Edfu and Heiraknopolis

MA'AT
For the Egyptians, the universe was based on order and harmony. The rising and setting of the Sun, the yearly flooding of the Nile River, and the course of the stars across the sky were all maintained by Ma'at, the goddess of order. She was often shown as a winged woman with an ostrich feather on her head.

Egyptians believed that if Ma'at didn't exist, the universe would

sink into chaos

Ma'at

Ma'at was the goddess of truth, justice, and order. In Egyptian mythology, the hearts of the dead were weighed against one of Ma'at's feathers. If the heart weighed the same as the feather, the dead would be reborn in the underworld.

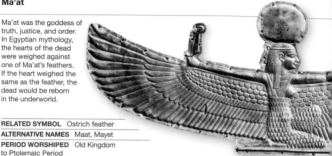

RELATED SYMBOL Ostrich feather

ALTERNATIVE NAMES Maat, Mayet

PERIOD WORSHIPED Old Kingdom to Ptolemaic Period

CENTER OF WORSHIP All Egyptian cities

Hathor

Hathor, whose name means "House of House," is seen in the 1st dynasty as a woman with the ears and horns of a cow. At Giza she was also the Mistress of the Sycamore tree and regarded as the divine mother of the king.

RELATED SYMBOL Cow

ALTERNATIVE NAMES None

PERIOD WORSHIPED Early Dynastic Period to Ptolemaic Period

CENTER OF WORSHIP Denderah

Khepri

Egyptians often saw scarabs, or dung beetles, rolling dung into a ball and pushing it across the ground. They associated this with Khepri, who rolled the Sun across the sky. This god was later merged with Ra and represented the rising Sun.

RELATED SYMBOL Scarab

ALTERNATIVE NAMES Kheper, Khepera, Chepri

PERIOD WORSHIPED Old Kingdom to Ptolemaic Period

CENTER OF WORSHIP Heliopolis

Wadjet

In Pre-dynastic times, Wadjet was worshiped as the patron goddess of Lower Egypt. She later merged with the cat-goddess Bastet and was shown with the head of a lioness.

RELATED SYMBOL Cobra

ALTERNATIVE NAMES Wadjit, Buto

PERIOD WORSHIPED
Old Kingdom to Ptolemaic Period

CENTER OF WORSHIP
Per-wadjet

Ra

The Sun god Ra was one of the most popular gods of Egyptian religion. He was represented by the disk of the Sun, but in many places he was combined with local gods to make a powerful deity. One such deity was Ra-Harakhty, who was a combination of Ra and the sky-god Horus.

Ra-Harakhty holding an Ankh, the Egyptian symbol for eternal life

RELATED SYMBOL Sun

ALTERNATIVE NAMES Re

PERIOD WORSHIPED Early Dynastic Period to Ptolemaic Period

CENTER OF WORSHIP Heliopolis

Isis once tricked Ra into revealing his secret name. This allowed her to become pregnant with Horus even after her husband's death.

Seshat

The goddess of writing and measurement, Seshat's name means, "she who writes." She was depicted as participating in the foundation of temples, making sure that the measurements were correct.

RELATED SYMBOL Seven-pointed star or flower on a pole

ALTERNATIVE NAMES Sesha, Sesheta, Safekh-Aubi

PERIOD WORSHIPED Old Kingdom to Ptolemaic Period

CENTER OF WORSHIP None

Sobek

Crocodile-headed Sobek was the god of rivers and lakes. His temple at Faiyum had a live crocodile named Petsuchos. His followers believed that the crocodile was Sobek himself and was therefore sacred.

RELATED SYMBOL Crocodile

ALTERNATIVE NAMES Sebek, Sebek-Ra, Sobeq

PERIOD WORSHIPED Old Kingdom to Ptolemaic Period

CENTER OF WORSHIP Kom Ombo

Thoth

The inventor of hieroglyphs, Thoth recorded the decision taken on the dead who were judged for rebirth. He also had a book containing all the wisdom in the world. Isis came to him when she needed a spell to bring Osiris back to life. This wall painting shows Queen Nefertari asking Thoth for a writing palette.

RELATED SYMBOL Ibis or baboon

ALTERNATIVE NAMES Tehuty, Djehuty, Tahuti

PERIOD WORSHIPED Old Kingdom to Ptolemaic Period

CENTER OF WORSHIP Khnum (Hermopolis)

Amun

Amun was part of a group of eight gods called the Ogdoad of Hermopolis. Other members of this group were Heh and Hauhet, who represented eternity. The name Amun means "the hidden one." It was thought that he created himself and then the universe, while remaining distant and separate from it. This statue is from the New Kingdom, when Amun was merged with the Sun god Ra and adopted into the Ennead of Heliopolis as Amun-Ra.

RELATED SYMBOL Ram or goose

ALTERNATIVE NAMES Amen, Ammon

PERIOD WORSHIPED Middle Kingdom to Late Period

CENTER OF WORSHIP Thebes

Bastet

Originally taking the shape of a desert cat or a lioness, Bastet was a fierce deity. She was the daughter of Ra and represented the power of the Sun to ripen crops. Around 1500 BCE, Egyptians began domesticating cats. Bastet then came to be seen as kinder and was worshiped in the form of a cat or a woman with a cat's head.

RELATED SYMBOL Cat
ALTERNATIVE NAMES Bast
PERIOD WORSHIPED Old Kingdom to Late Period
CENTER OF WORSHIP Bubastis

Taweret

With the head of a hippopotamus, the limbs of a lion, and the body of a human, Taweret had a strange appearance. She was also sometimes shown with the tail of a crocodile. She was worshiped as the goddess of childbirth.

RELATED SYMBOL Hippopotamus
ALTERNATIVE NAMES Taueret, Tawaret, Taurt
PERIOD WORSHIPED New Kingdom to Late Period
CENTER OF WORSHIP Jabal al-Silsila

Apep

Bes

A household god, Bes was the protector of women and newborn babies. It was said that if a baby smiled or laughed for no reason, it was because Bes was making funny faces.

RELATED SYMBOL
Dwarf god

ALTERNATIVE NAMES
Bisu, Aha

PERIOD WORSHIPED
New Kingdom to
Ptolemaic Period

CENTER OF WORSHIP
Homes

The serpent god of chaos, Apep was always locked away in the underworld. However, this did not stop him from waging a constant battle against the Sun god, Ra. He attacked Ra every day, but was defeated each time. This painting shows Ra, in the form of a cat, killing Apep.

RELATED SYMBOL Serpent

ALTERNATIVE NAMES Apophis

PERIOD WORSHIPED
New Kingdom

CENTER OF WORSHIP None

Aten

In Akhenaten's reign, only the Sun god Aten was worshiped. The god was depicted as the Sun's disk with rays that touched with human hands. Aten was probably the only Egyptian god who was not represented in a human or humanlike form.

RELATED SYMBOL Sun disk with rays ending as hands

ALTERNATIVE NAMES None

PERIOD WORSHIPED Not worshipped

CENTER OF WORSHIP Akhetaten (Amarna)

The "opening of the mouth" ceremony
magically enabled the mummy to

breathe and speak

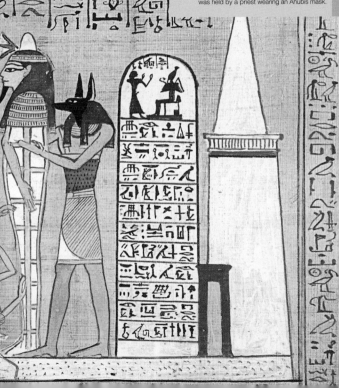

BRINGING BACK TO LIFE
The "opening of the mouth" was a ritual associated with mummification. During the ceremony, special tools were held to the mummy's mouth, including adzes, blades, and the foreleg of a bull. The mummy was held by a priest wearing an Anubis mask.

Temples

Egyptian temples were designed to be imposing structures. They had massive stone walls and rows of columns carved with religious images and hieroglyphs. Since a temple was considered the home of a god, ordinary people could only enter the outer court. Priests performed sacred rituals in dark rooms at the heart of the temple.

Sun temple of Niuserre

This was one of the many Sun temples built during the 5th Dynasty. It was originally built using mud bricks, but was later rebuilt entirely with stone. A stone path connects the temple to the pyramid of Niuserre.

DEDICATED TO Ra

BUILT IN 5th Dynasty Old Kingdom

LOCATION Abu Gurab

Temple of Hathor, Abu Simbel

The temple of Hathor at Abu Simbel was built by Ramesses II to honor Nefertari, his chief royal wife. The entire face of a stone hill was carved into giant statues of Ramesses II and Nefertari. Chambers inside the temple depict the royal couple making offerings to the gods.

DEDICATED TO Hathor

BUILT IN 1279–1213 BCE
(19th Dynasty New Kingdom)

LOCATION Abu Simbel, Nubia

Karnak temple complex

This temple complex began as a small set of buildings dedicated to local gods during the 11th Dynasty. By the 19th Dynasty, it was a huge complex with more than 80,000 people working in it as servants, guards, and priests.

DEDICATED TO Amun-Ra

BUILT IN 11th Dynasty onward

LOCATION Karnak

Statue of Amun

Temple of Dakka

A small structure, this temple was built by Arkamanian, a Meroitic king, in 220 BCE. The Ptolemaic rulers later added more buildings, such as a gate and a columned porch.

DEDICATED TO Thoth

BUILT IN Ptolemaic Period

LOCATION New Wadi es-Sebua

Kom Ombo temple

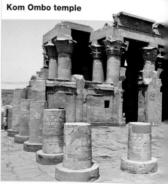

Luxor temple

The Luxor temple is built on the eastern bank of the Nile River. The first phase was built by Amenhotep III. Pharaoh Ramesses II made many additions to the temple, building monuments such as this obelisk. Over the centuries, the temple was buried under sand and silt. This helped preserve its structures until it was excavated in 1881 CE.

DEDICATED TO Amun

BUILT IN c.1400 BCE (18th–19th Dynasty New Kingdom)

LOCATION Luxor

The obelisk is made of red granite and weighs more than 250 tons (227 metric tonnes)

The Kom Ombo temple is unique among the temples of ancient Egypt as it is dedicated to two gods—Sobek and Horus. The building has two entrances, two halls, and two sanctuaries. The left side of the temple is for Horus, while the right side is for Sobek.

DEDICATED TO Sobek and Horus

BUILT IN Ptolemaic Period

LOCATION Kom Ombo

Mortuary temple of Hatshepsut

Ancient Egyptians believed that the pharaohs became gods after death. To worship them, buildings called mortuary temples were built near their tombs. Designed by Pharaoh Hatshepsut's architect Senenmut, this temple is an extraordinary monument that rises from the desert plain in a series of grand terraces connected by long ramps.

DEDICATED TO Amun-Ra

BUILT IN 1470 BCE (18th Dynasty New Kingdom)

LOCATION Deir el-Bahari

Temple of Derr

Cut deep into rock, the Temple of Derr was built in the 30th year of Ramesses II's reign. Ancient Egyptians named it the "Temple of Ramesses–in-the-house-of-Ra." Early Christians converted it into a church and removed many of the decorations that covered the walls and roof.

DEDICATED TO Ra-Harakhty

BUILT IN 19th Dynasty New Kingdom

LOCATION Eastern bank of Nile in lower Nubia

Thutmose III, the pharaoh after Hatshepsut, erased all references to her in the temple, replacing them with his own name.

Temple of Amada

This is the oldest surviving Egyptian temple in Nubia and was constructed by Thutmosis III and Amenhotep II. Paintings and wall carvings inside the temple show the pharaohs making offerings to the gods.

DEDICATED TO Amun

BUILT IN 18th Dynasty New Kingdom

LOCATION Amada

Temple of Wadi es-Sebua

Wadi es-Sebua means "the valley of lions." The temple was so named because it had an avenue of sphinxes lining its approach. The temple is decorated with two colossi and many smaller statues of its builder, Ramesses II.

DEDICATED TO Amun-Ra

BUILT IN 1244–1229 BCE (19th Dynasty New Kingdom)

LOCATION Wadi es-Sebua, Lower Nubia

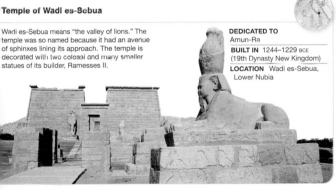

Temple of Hathor at Dendera

Dendera was the cult center of Hathor from Pre-dynastic times. The main hall of this temple has 18 columns, each decorated with the head of the goddess.

DEDICATED TO Hathor

BUILT IN 2250–343 BCE (6th–30th Dynasties Old Kingdom to to Roman Period)

LOCATION Dendera

Temple of Philae

As the center of the cult of Isis, the Temple of Philae was a place of pilgrimage for her worshipers. After the building of the Aswan Dam in the 1960s, parts of the temple were submerged under water. Between 1972 and 1980, the entire temple was moved to the island of Agilkia.

DEDICATED TO Isis

BUILT IN 380–362 BCE (26th Dynasty to Roman Period)

LOCATION Agilkia island, near Aswan

Deir el-Shelwit

This small structure was built while Egypt was ruled by the Roman Empire. The outer wall of the temple was constructed of material reused from New Kingdom buildings.

DEDICATED TO Isis

BUILT IN 1st century CE

LOCATION Luxor

Temple of Gorf Hussein

This temple was built by Setau, who was the Viceroy of Nubia. It was named Per Ptah, which means "the House of Ptah." The hall of the temple is decorated with standing statues of Ramesses II.

DEDICATED TO Ptah and Hathor

BUILT IN 1279–1213 BCE
(19th Dynasty New Kingdom)

LOCATION Built at lower Nubia, moved to a site near Aswan due to the construction of the Aswan Dam

Statue of Ramesses II holding crook and flail

Small Temple of Aten

The Small Temple of Aten was built by Akhenaten as part of his city of Akhetaten. Like much of the city, the temple was built using mudbricks, sandstone, and limestone plaster.

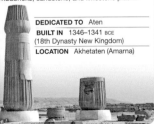

DEDICATED TO Aten

BUILT IN 1346–1341 BCE
(18th Dynasty New Kingdom)

LOCATION Akhetaten (Amarna)

Sacred artifacts

In ancient Egypt, only priests and royalty could enter the rooms and shrines inside a temple. Priests performed rituals to please the gods. The objects used in these rituals were sacred, often representing the gods themselves.

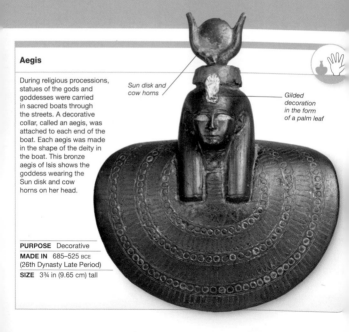

Aegis

During religious processions, statues of the gods and goddesses were carried in sacred boats through the streets. A decorative collar, called an aegis, was attached to each end of the boat. Each aegis was made in the shape of the deity in the boat. This bronze aegis of Isis shows the goddess wearing the Sun disk and cow horns on her head.

Sun disk and cow horns

Gilded decoration in the form of a palm leaf

PURPOSE Decorative
MADE IN 685–525 BCE
(26th Dynasty Late Period)
SIZE 3¾ in (9.65 cm) tall

Copper standard

Egyptian priests carried standards, or poles, in their processions through temples. All that has survived of these are the emblems on top of the poles. This emblem shows Horus in the form of a falcon. He is wearing the combined crowns of Upper and Lower Egypt on his head.

PURPOSE Processions

MADE IN 685–525 BCE (26th Dynasty Late Period)

SIZE 7¼ in (18.5 cm) tall

Situla

This bronze container held water from a sacred lake. Such lakes were a part of every temple complex. The situla was used to sprinkle holy water during religious rituals.

Bucket is decorated with images of gods and pharaohs

PURPOSE Carrying water

MADE IN Late Period

SIZE 10 in (25 cm) tall

Cult mirror

A temple was considered to be the home of a deity. So everyday objects, such as mirrors, were placed in temples for the deities to use. This is the cult mirror of the Moon god Khonsu. The face of the mirror is covered with different religious symbols.

PURPOSE Mirror for deity

MADE IN New Kingdom

SIZE 14½ in (37 cm) long

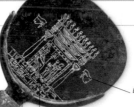

Eye of Horus

Mut, Khonsu's mother, receiving offerings from a priest

Head of Khonsu on top of handle

Corn mummy

Egyptians saw the growth of a plant from a tiny seed as a symbol of rebirth, or resurrection. During the annual festival for Osiris, the god of resurrection, they made small mummies out of clay, sand, and corn seeds. These were then wrapped and put in coffins, which were placed in tombs as offerings to Osiris.

Coffin lid is decorated with images of deities

PURPOSE
Offering
MADE IN
Roman Period
SIZE 22 in
(56 cm) tall

Ibis mummy case

This gold container holds the mummified body of an ibis. Ibises were the sacred animals of Thoth. His worshipers often paid to get such mummies made as offerings to him.

PURPOSE Container
MADE IN Roman Period
SIZE 13½ in (34 cm) long

Feet are made of bronze

Crocodile mummy

The god of rivers and lakes, Sobek was represented by a crocodile. His priests even kept tame crocodiles in his temples. These reptiles were fed the best meats and wine. When a crocodile died, it was mummified and buried as an offering to Sobek.

Reeds used to pad out crocodile shape

Four million mummified ibises were discovered in an animal cemetery at Tuna El-gebel.

Cat mummy

Cats were sacred animals of the goddess Bastet and were kept in her temples. When these cats died, they were mummified, wrapped in linen cloth, and placed in cat-shaped coffins. It was considered a holy act for temple visitors to buy the coffins and have them buried.

PURPOSE	Offering
MADE IN	Roman Period
SIZE	18 in (46 cm) tall

PURPOSE	Offering
MADE IN	Roman Period
SIZE	37 in (94 cm) long

Bulge of crocodile's eye can be seen through wrapping

Apis bull statuette

The Apis bull was worshiped as the living form of Osiris. When an Apis bull died, it was embalmed and buried in a massive stone sarcophagus in a temple called Serapeum. Worshipers often donated small sculptures, such as the one below, as offerings to the bull.

Sun disk between horns

PURPOSE	Offering
MADE IN	Ptolemaic Period
SIZE	5½ in (14 cm) long

RESCUE EFFORT
To save the Temple of Philae from being submerged, a dam was built around the entire island, and the inside was pumped dry. Then the temple was taken apart and rebuilt on the island of Agilkia, which was completely reshaped to resemble Philae.

The Temple of Philae was dismantled into **40,000 blocks,** which, together, weighed about 20,000 tons

Daily life

The lives of ancient Egyptians were closely linked to the Nile River. Farmers worked on the flood plain of the river, growing wheat, barley, fruits, and vegetables. Mud from the river was used to make household utensils, such as pots and spoons. Hunting wildlife around the river was a popular sport of the upper classes, as seen in the tomb painting on the left. It shows a nobleman and his family out on a bird hunt.

TERRA-COTTA BOTTLE
A type of hard-baked clay, terra-cotta was used widely in ancient Egypt. This terra-cotta bottle is shaped like a mother and her baby and was used to store milk.

Daily life

The common people of ancient Egypt worked as farmers or craftworkers, playing music and board games in their spare time. They usually wore linen clothes and makeup made from minerals.

Craftworkers

Using a variety of tools, such as drills, axes, and chisels, Egyptian craftworkers made many beautiful objects out of wood, gold, silver, and faïence.

Carpenters using tools such as saws, chisels, and hammers

Model of carpentry workshop found in tomb

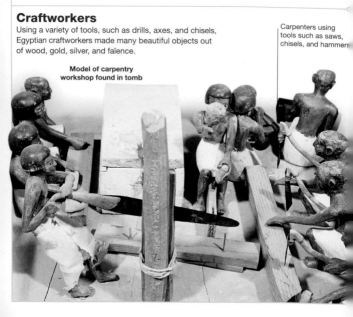

Farming

The tomb painting on the left shows an Egyptian farmer cutting stalks of grain with a sickle. After cutting it, the farmer would clean the grain and store it in a large mud-brick granary.

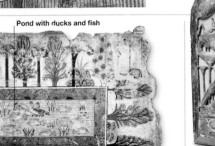

Pond with ducks and fish

Painting of wealthy Egyptian's villa with garden

Living

Houses were made of mud bricks, with narrow windows to keep the Sun's heat out. Wealthy families lived in large villas with gardens and pools, while poorer people lived in simple homes.

Hunting

This shield shows Pharaoh Tutankhamun hunting and killing two lions. Hunting was popular with royalty and noblemen, as a way to show strength and courage.

Egyptians at home

Egyptians lived in houses made of mud bricks. Among the peasants, both men and women worked in the fields, while in wealthier families, the women stayed at home and the men worked as traders or officials.

FOCUS ON...
FOOD
An Egyptian meal included bread and vegetables, along with beer or wine.

Model of bread-making

Bread was an important part of the Egyptian diet. Bread-making was a tiring job, since it required kneeling down and grinding grain into flour for hours, as shown in the model below. Dirt or sand would get into the flour while it was being ground, making the bread hard and gritty. This caused damage to the teeth.

MADE IN
Middle Kingdom

SIZE 16¾ in (42.5 cm) wide

Model of Egyptian house

Models of houses were placed in tombs so that the dead could have a house in their next life. These were known as soul-houses. This model shows the house of a poor family. The house has a walled courtyard with models of food items, including meat and loaves of bread, placed in it.

MADE IN
12th Dynasty
Middle Kingdom

SIZE 16¼ in (40.6 cm) long

◀ Egyptians ate bread with every meal. Bread was made of barley, wheat, and figs.

▲ The date palm tree was thought to be sacred and its fruit was placed as an offering in tombs.

▲ Figs were either eaten fresh or used as a sweetener.

Wine jar

Wine and beer were two of the main drinks of ancient Egypt. Beer was drunk by everyone, but wine was usually used in religious ceremonies and drunk by the rich. This wine jar was probably used in the house of a wealthy family. Its narrow base shows that it would have been set on a stand or held by a servant.

MADE IN 21st Dynasty
Third Intermediate Period

SIZE 9¼ in
(23.5 cm) long

Clothes and cloth

Egyptians wore simple clothes made of linen. Men wore short skirts, called kilts, with a cloak around their shoulders. Women wore long, tight-fitting dresses. Both men and women wore wigs.

Wig

Wigs were used on public occasions and in religious ceremonies. This wig is made from 300 strands of actual human hair, each strand containing 400 hairs. The curly hair at the top has been strengthened with beeswax and resin.

MADE IN 18th Dynasty New Kingdom

SIZE 19¾ in (49.5 cm) long

Linen cloth

The types of linen available in Egypt ranged from coarse cloth worn by the poor, to fine gauze, which was worn by royalty. This piece of cloth has a pattern stitched on it in linen thread.

MADE IN Middle Kingdom

SIZE 4 in (10 cm) long

Spindle

Spindles were used to spin fiber into threads, which were then woven on a loom. This spindle was weighed down by a stone wheel or whorl.

MADE IN Middle Kingdom

SIZE 14½ in (37 cm) long

Fiber strands were twisted around spindle

Stone whorl

Leather sandals

Egyptians usually walked barefoot and wore footwear only on special occasions. The sandals worn by the poor were made of woven papyrus reeds, while those worn by the rich were made of leather or wood. These sandals were recovered from the tomb of Pharaoh Tutankhamun. They are made of wood and decorated with leather and gold leaf.

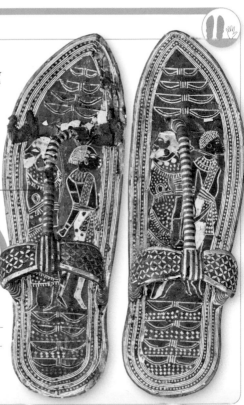

Figure of enemy soldier painted on sandal

Every time a pharaoh wore his sandals, he would symbolically trample on his enemies, who were depicted on the shoes.

MADE IN 18th Dynasty New Kingdom

SIZE 11 in (28 cm) long

Toys and games

Egyptian children played with balls, dolls, and toy animals, just as children do today. Adults preferred to play board games, such as senet and mehen. In fact, Tutankhamun liked senet so much that he was buried with four complete sets of the game to play in the afterlife.

Mehen (snake game)

This was one of the earliest known multiplayer board games played in Egypt. The board was in the shape of a coiled snake, which represented the god Mehen, who protected the Sun god Ra from his enemies. Players started at the tip of the snake's tail and moved their counters around the squares on the snake's body to the middle. The counters were sometimes carved with the names of Egypt's earliest pharaohs.

MADE IN Early Dynastic Old Kingdom

SIZE 14½ in (37 cm) wide

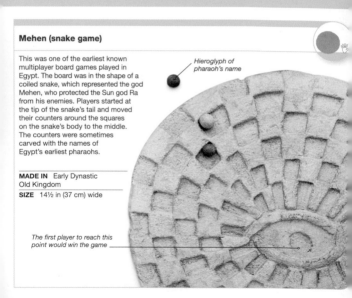

Hieroglyph of pharaoh's name

The first player to reach this point would win the game

Toy mouse

Ancient Egyptians used a variety of materials to make toys, including wood, bone, ivory, ceramics, and stone. Toys were modeled on objects, people, and animals that were common in everyday life. This wooden mouse had a string attached to its tail, which could be pulled to make the tail go up and down.

MADE IN New Kingdom

SIZE 3 in (7.5 cm) long (including tail)

Throwsticks

Throwsticks were used in Egypt in much the same way dice are used today. These sticks could be made of reed, wood, bone, or ivory, and were painted with different colors to tell the sides apart.

MADE IN 1500–1069 BCE (18th–20th Dynasty New Kingdom)

SIZE 7 in (18 cm) long

Senet

The game of senet symbolized a person's struggle against the forces of evil, which tried to prevent him or her from reaching the kingdom of Osiris. The game board had 30 squares. Some squares were dangerous to land on, others were lucky. The winner was believed to be protected by the gods.

MADE IN 1400–1200 BCE (18th–19th Dynasty New Kingdom)

SIZE 11 in (28 cm) long

Game counter

Painted toy horse

Only the wealthy owned horses in ancient Egypt. The animals were considered status symbols and were often given as gifts to the rulers of other kingdoms. This wooden horse was pulled along by a rope that was threaded through its muzzle.

MADE IN Roman Period

SIZE 4½ in (11 cm) long

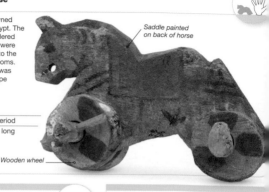

Saddle painted on back of horse

Wooden wheel

Dogs and jackals

In addition to mehen and senet, another popular board game was the game of dogs and jackals. The goal was to complete a circuit of the board before the other player. This board is shaped like a hippopotamus.

MADE IN 525–332 BCE (27th–30th Dynasty Late Period)

SIZE 8¾ in (21.5 cm) long

Wooden cat

This wooden toy is carved roughly into the shape of a cat. Pulling the string makes its lower jaw move up and down. It has bronze teeth and pieces of rock crystal for eyes.

Painted balls

These balls are made of linen and strengthened by reeds. They are hollow and were originally filled with seeds or small beads of clay, which made the balls rattle when thrown or caught.

MADE IN Roman Period

SIZE 2½ in (6.6 cm) wide

MADE IN New Kingdom

SIZE 4¾ in (11.7 cm) long

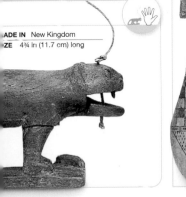

Wooden doll

Dolls in ancient Egypt were made of wood, clay, ivory, linen, or papyrus. This wooden doll has hair made of clay beads attached to twine or string. Some believe that such dolls were only used as toys, but others argue that they were put in tombs as companions for the afterlife.

MADE IN First Intermediate Period to Middle Kingdom

SIZE 7½ in (19.1 cm) long

Painted dress of red, yellow, and black squares

Music

Vital to Egyptian life, music was played during celebrations, religious festivals, and even during everyday work. Noblewomen would play the harp to help their husbands relax, while farmers would sing to their oxen to make them work better.

FOCUS ON...
MUSICIANS
Professional musician were present in many different levels of Egyptian society.

Sistrum

The sistrum was mainly associated with the goddess Hathor. Noblewomen and priestesses carried it at religious ceremonies. Small metal rings on the crossbars would move when the sistrum shook, producing a rattling sound.

Metal rings

Handle decorated with the head of Hathor

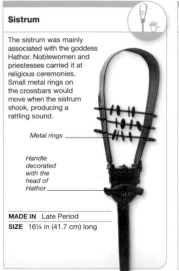

MADE IN Late Period

SIZE 16¼ in (41.7 cm) long

Harp

The harps played in ancient Egypt varied greatly in size, shape, and the number of strings. This five-stringed harp was found in the tomb of an Egyptian named Ani. The design of the pharaoh head on it suggests that it belonged to a court musician.

Head of Horus

Peg for tuning string

MADE IN New Kingdom

SIZE 38 in (97 cm) total length

◄ This painting shows Egyptian musicians playing harps, lyres, and flutes. Among musicians, the ones who played in temples had the highest status. Mainly women, they were given the title *Shemayet*, meaning "musician." Next came the musicians of the royal court, who included gifted singers and harp players. There were also groups of musicians who traveled from place to place as troupes, playing at banquets and festivals.

End of harp is carved in the shape of a pharaoh wearing a Nemes headdress

Clappers

Clappers were used in Egyptian music in the same way as modern castanets. Musicians held the clappers in one hand and banged them together. Made of ivory and bone, these clappers were held together by a piece of string.

MADE IN 1991–1902 BCE (12th Dynasty Middle Kingdom)

SIZE 6½ in (17 cm) long

Clapper is carved to look like a hand

Hunting and fishing

Farming and livestock provided people with enough food, so hunting was mainly done as a sport. Egyptians hunted wild bulls, gazelles, lions, crocodiles, and hippopotamuses. Bird hunting was also popular among noblemen. Fishing, on the other hand, was done both for food and for fun.

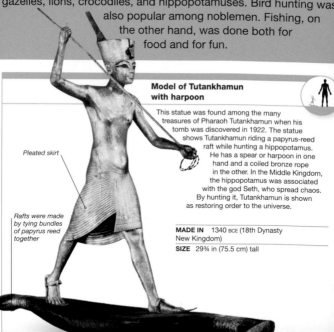

Pleated skirt

Rafts were made by tying bundles of papyrus reed together

Model of Tutankhamun with harpoon

This statue was found among the many treasures of Pharaoh Tutankhamun when his tomb was discovered in 1922. The statue shows Tutankhamun riding a papyrus-reed raft while hunting a hippopotamus. He has a spear or harpoon in one hand and a coiled bronze rope in the other. In the Middle Kingdom, the hippopotamus was associated with the god Seth, who spread chaos. By hunting it, Tutankhamun is shown as restoring order to the universe.

MADE IN 1340 BCE (18th Dynasty New Kingdom)

SIZE 29¾ in (75.5 cm) tall

Arrow

Ancient Egyptians were skilled archers. They made arrows from the reeds that grew on the banks of the Nile River. The arrowheads were made of ivory, bone, flint, obsidian, or metal. The sharp tip of this bronze arrowhead could pierce through an animal's skin, injuring it severely.

MADE IN Late Period
SIZE 4¼ in (10.6 cm) long

Barb at end of arrow prevented it from being pulled out easily

Throwing stick

Shaped like boomerangs, these wooden throwing sticks were used to hunt wildfowl. The hunter would use a boat to approach the reeds where the birds were resting. When they emerged, he would hurl a stick at them in the hope of breaking their necks or wings, or at least stunning them.

MADE IN New Kingdom
SIZE 23 in (59 cm) long

Throwing sticks were also used in battle as weapons for hitting enemy soldiers from far away.

Fishing hook

During the Old Kingdom, fish were usually caught in nets or by using spears. Later, fishermen began using bronze hooks, such as this one, to catch fish. These hooks were attached by a string to a pole. When a fish caught a hook in its mouth, it would tug the string and the fisherman would pull it out of the water.

MADE IN New Kingdom
SIZE 1¼ in (3 cm) long

Farming

The Nile River flooded between July and September. When the floods ended, the banks of the river were covered with rich fertile soil. Farmers planted their crops in October and harvested them between March and May. The main crops were wheat, barley, and flax, but farmers also grew beans, lentils, onions, leeks, cucumbers, and lettuce.

Granary model

Ancient Egyptians used granaries to store grain. These buildings were made of mud bricks, which protected the grain from rodents and insects. This model shows workers storing grain inside the building, while a scribe is recording the amount being stored.

MADE IN Middle Kingdom

SIZE 17 in (43 cm) long

People often placed models of granaries in tombs, hoping to provide an unlimited supply of food in the afterlife.

Farmer model

In this model, the figure of the farmer is guiding the oxen as they drag a simple wooden plow behind them. The soil on the Nile flood plain was soft, allowing the farmers to plow it easily.

MADE IN 1985–1795 BCE
(12th Dynasty Middle Kingdom)

SIZE 17 in (43 cm) long

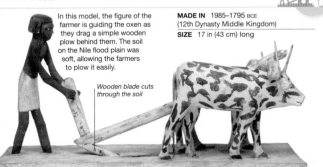

Wooden blade cuts through the soil

Winnowing fan

After the grain was harvested, it was winnowed, or separated, from its husk. The workers would gather up the grain in wooden, winnowing fans and throw it into the air. The lighter husks would blow away, leaving the grain to fall to the floor.

MADE IN New Kingdom

SIZE 19 in (48 cm) long

Raised edge of winnowing fan prevented grain from spilling out

Sickle

This simple sickle is made of wood and flint. The sharp pieces of flint attached to the blade allowed farmers to cut the stalks of grain during harvest. The stalks left behind were later gathered to make mats and baskets.

MADE IN 18th Dynasty
New Kingdom

SIZE 11¼ in (28.5 cm) long

Cutting edge made of flint

CATTLE COUNT
In ancient Egypt, an event called the cattle count took place every year, to calculate a person's wealth. This model was found in the tomb of Meketre, an Egyptian nobleman. He is shown sitting in his courtyard while four scribes count his cattle.

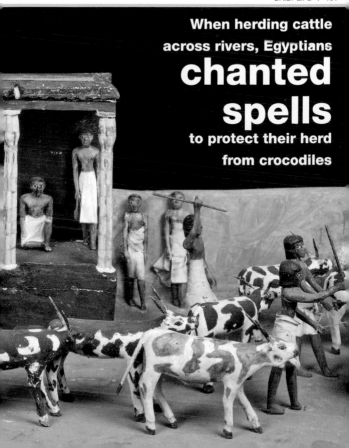

When herding cattle across rivers, Egyptians **chanted spells** to protect their herd from crocodiles

Boats

The Nile River was the main highway of Egypt. Everything, from grain and cattle to coffins and building blocks, was transported by water. The earliest boats were made of bundles of papyrus reeds and propelled using oars. By 3000 BCE, Egyptians began building timber boats and using the wind to sail on the river.

Model of fishing skiffs

This is a model of two Egyptian boats called fishing skiffs. Such boats were made of papyrus, which made them easy to carry as well as to repair. In this model, the skiffs have a net stretched between them. As the boats move forward, fish are caught in the net and then pulled out.

MADE IN 12th Dynasty Middle Kingdom
SIZE 24½ in (62 cm) long

The Egyptians believed that the Sun god Ra himself traveled across the sky in a papyrus skiff.

Model of funeral boat

The Egyptians placed boats or models of boats in tombs because they believed that the dead were taken to the Underworld by boat. This model boat has two female mourners to accompany the mummy. The green color of the boat symbolizes rebirth in the afterlife.

MADE IN 12th Dynasty Middle Kingdom

SIZE 26 in (66.7 cm) long

Small statue of a mummy

Model of sailboat

Mostly used for transportation, sailboats were bigger than fishing boats. They had one square sail and were steered by two oars. This model sailboat was found in a tomb at Beni-Hasan, a cemetery on the eastern bank of the Nile. The sail and mast were missing and replacements were added based on other boats found at Thebes.

Square sail

Oar for changing boat's direction

MADE IN Around 2000 BCE (12th Dynasty Middle Kingdom)

SIZE 4 ft (1.2 m) long

Magic and medicine

Ancient Egyptians had great faith in magic and medicine. It was a common belief that wearing magical amulets could ward off any dangers that might threaten people or their families. Egyptian doctors wrote many manuals that described how to treat a variety of ailments, such as fevers, tumors, and eye disorders.

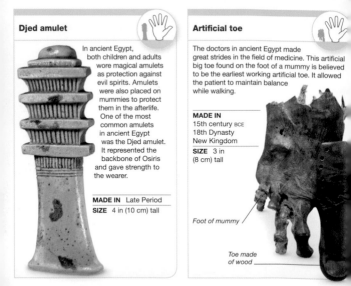

Djed amulet

In ancient Egypt, both children and adults wore magical amulets as protection against evil spirits. Amulets were also placed on mummies to protect them in the afterlife. One of the most common amulets in ancient Egypt was the Djed amulet. It represented the backbone of Osiris and gave strength to the wearer.

MADE IN Late Period
SIZE 4 in (10 cm) tall

Artificial toe

The doctors in ancient Egypt made great strides in the field of medicine. This artificial big toe found on the foot of a mummy is believed to be the earliest working artificial toe. It allowed the patient to maintain balance while walking.

MADE IN
15th century BCE
18th Dynasty
New Kingdom
SIZE 3 in
(8 cm) tall

Foot of mummy

Toe made of wood

Prayer stela

Placed in houses as a protection against dangers, stelae were stone tablets with prayers on them addressed to the gods. This stela shows a prayer to Horus to protect the family from danger. Pictured in human form as a child, Horus is shown trampling two crocodiles, while gripping snakes, lions, and scorpions in his hand. These animals were not only signs of ill omens, but also real threats that were present in the desert.

— *Magic spells cover the stela's sides*

MADE IN Ptolemaic Period

SIZE 10 in (26 cm) tall

Amuletic wand

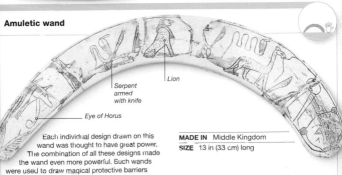

Serpent armed with knife

Lion

— *Eye of Horus*

Each individual design drawn on this wand was thought to have great power. The combination of all these designs made the wand even more powerful. Such wands were used to draw magical protective barriers around parts of a house.

MADE IN Middle Kingdom

SIZE 13 in (33 cm) long

Tools

Egyptian workers built giant structures using the simplest of tools. At first, tools were made of copper, which is a soft metal, so they would get blunt quickly. Later, Egyptians began using bronze, which is stronger than copper and stayed sharper.

Adze

Adzes are tools used to cut and trim rough planks of wood and to shape and level wooden surfaces. Egyptian carpenters used them to build ships and make intricate wooden objects, such as chests, chairs, and even figurines. This adze was found in the tomb of Ani in Thebes.

Wooden handle

MADE IN New Kingdom

SIZE 25½ in (64.8 cm) long

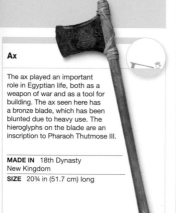

Ax

The ax played an important role in Egyptian life, both as a weapon of war and as a tool for building. The ax seen here has a bronze blade, which has been blunted due to heavy use. The hieroglyphs on the blade are an inscription to Pharaoh Thutmose III.

MADE IN 18th Dynasty New Kingdom

SIZE 20¾ in (51.7 cm) long

Leather straps join blade to handle

Bronze blade

Smoother

Once built, the walls of houses and tombs in ancient Egypt were coated with plaster. A smoother, such as the one shown below, flattened the plaster, creating a plain surface on which paintings could be made.

MADE IN New Kingdom
SIZE 6½ in (17 cm) long

Chisel

Masons use chisels to work on stone. In ancient Egypt, fine details in reliefs, sculptures, and monuments were carved out using copper and bronze chisels. The tips of the chisels were sometimes heated to make it easier to cut the stone.

MADE IN Late Period
SIZE 6¾ in (17.5 cm) long

Bow drill

Egyptian workers used bow drills to make holes in wood and stone. A worker would wrap the the string of the bow around the drill holder, and move the bow back and forth to turn the metal drill fast enough to bore holes. The holder of this drill is well-worn, suggesting that the owner had used it a lot.

Drill holder

Wooden bow

Metal drill

MADE IN New Kingdom
SIZE 18½ in (47 cm) long

Jewelry

The craftworkers of ancient Egypt used many different materials to create beautiful pieces of jewelry. These materials included gold, silver, ivory, glass, and faïence. Egyptian jewelry was not only used for simple decoration, but also in official seals and to make lucky charms.

Bracelet of Nimlot

Sheet of beaten gold

This bracelet was made for Nimlot, son of Pharaoh Sheshonq I. The central design shows the god Horus as a child sitting on a lotus flower. Like many children in Egyptian art, the god is shown sucking his thumb. The hieroglyphs on the inside of the bracelet spell the owner's name. The bracelet was found at Sais, an important city during the Third Intermediate Period.

MADE IN 940 BCE (22nd Dynasty Third Intermediate Period)

SIZE 2½ in (6.3 cm) across

Falcon pectoral

A pectoral was a type of jewelry worn on the chest. This falcon pectoral was designed using a framework of metal cells that were filled with segments of faïence, glass, and gems. This technique is called cloisonné.

MADE IN 1370 BCE (18th Dynasty New Kingdom)

SIZE 6½ in (16 cm) wide

Metal plate shaped as wing

Traces of original inlay

Lucky girdle

Egyptian jewelers used an alloy called electrum—a mixture of gold and silver—in jewelry. The lucky charms on this girdle, or belt, were made of electrum and strung on papyrus twine, along with beads of amethyst, coral, lapis lazuli, and turquoise.

MADE IN 2055–1650 BCE
(11th–14th Dynasty Middle Kingdom)

SIZE 18½ in (47 cm) long

Cowrie shell to bring fertility

Lapis lazuli bead

Coral bead

Sidelocks to represent youth

Fish amulet to protect against drowning

Heh, god of "millions of years," symbolizes long life

Glass earring

Glass was also used to make jewelry, such as this earring. The purple and white edge of the earring was made by twisting strands of white and purple glass together. The ends of the earring are in the form of two loops, which held the wire that passed through the earlobe.

MADE IN 1550–1292 BCE
(18th Dynasty New Kingdom)

SIZE ¾ in (2 cm) diameter

Ring of Horemheb

Not all jewelry was made for display only. This ring bears the seal of Pharaoh Horemheb. It was probably used to stamp his official documents. The ring bears a cartouche with the hieroglyphs of Horemheb's name.

MADE IN 1323–1295 BCE
(19th Dynasty New Kingdom)

SIZE 1½ in (3.85 cm) diameter

Grooming

Personal appearance was very important to the Egyptians, and they went to great lengths to look beautiful. Many of the objects they used, such as combs, mirrors, and makeup, survive today.

FOCUS ON...
MAKEUP
Egyptians used pigments made from minerals for makeup.

Mirror

Most Egyptian men and women used mirrors made of copper or bronze. However, mirrors for royalty were made of polished silver. The owner of this silver mirror was Princess Sat-Hathor Yunet, daughter of Senusret II. The handle of the mirror is made of obsidian, a type of natural glass.

Handle is decorated with the face of the goddess Hathor, who was linked with beauty

MADE IN 1991–1802 BCE
(12th Dynasty Middle Kingdom)
SIZE 11 in (28 cm) long

Cosmetic jar

Men and women wore creams and perfumed oils not only to look beautiful, but also to prevent sunburn and damage from the sandy winds that blew in from the desert. These cosmetics were stored in this duck-shaped container.

MADE IN 1350–1300 BCE
(18th Dynasty New Kingdom)
SIZE 7 in
(17.5 cm) long

▲ They used the mineral galena to make kohl, a black eye paint.

▲ They ground malachite, a mineral of copper, to make green eye paint.

▲ They made a pigment called red ocher out of a mineral of iron.

Knob holds cover in place

Wing of duck forms cover for container

Kohl tube

The ancient Egyptians believed that using kohl protected the eye against diseases and the harsh rays of the Sun. They made kohl by grinding galena into a powder and mixing it with water to make a fine paste. This paste was stored inside narrow tubes, and applied to eyebrows, eyelashes, and eyelids using a thin stick.

Glass tube

MADE IN 1375–1275 BCE (19th Dynasty New Kingdom)

SIZE 3½ in (8.7 cm) long

EGYPTIAN FEAST
The Egyptians held feasts to celebrate birth, marriage, and religious festivals, or even just to entertain their friends. The cooks prepared huge meals consisting of cakes sweetened with honey and different kinds of meat, such as ibis, goose, and antelope, flavored with herbs and spices.

Guests at Egyptian feasts were entertained by
dancers, singers, and acrobats

Fascinating facts

TALLEST PYRAMIDS

❶ The Great Pyramid of Giza is the largest stone structure ever built. It is 482 ft (147 m) tall and weighs about 7.15 million tons (6.5 million metric tonnes).

❷ Originally standing 472 ft (144 m) tall, the **Pyramid of Khafra** was only 11½ ft (3.5 m) smaller than the Great Pyramid of Giza. Over the years, its outer casing has been removed, leaving it only 447½ ft (136.4 m) high.

❸ The Red Pyramid was built by Pharaoh Sneferu. It was the first true pyramid to be built in Egypt and is 344 ft (105 m) tall.

❹ The Bent Pyramid was the second pyramid to be built by Sneferu. It rises to a height of 330 ft (100 m). In ancient Egypt, it was known as "The Shining Pyramid of the South."

❺ The Meidum Pyramid was originally built as an eight-story pyramid with a total height of 307 ft (93.5 m). Over the years, it has crumbled, leaving only three stories.

❻ The Pyramid of Senusret III has a core made of mud bricks, unlike all other pyramids, which have cores made of blocks of stone. The pyramid stands 256 ft (78 m) tall.

❼ The Pyramid of Amenemhat III was originally named "Amenemhat is Mighty" in ancient Egypt. It was also called the Black Pyramid because of its dark appearance. It was 246 ft (75 m) tall, but is now just a small hill of rubble.

❽ The Pyramid of Neferirkare was the tallest structure built in Egypt during the 5th Dynasty. It reached a height of 230 ft (70 m).

❾ The Step Pyramid was the first pyramid ever built, almost 5,000 years ago. Unlike true pyramids, its sides are not of equal length. Its total height is 197 ft (60 m).

❿ The Pyramid of Senusret I was named "Senusret looks down on both lands" because it was built on top of a hill. The pyramid reached a height of 201 ft (61.25 m).

Pyramids were also built in ancient Greece and by the Aztecs and the Maya in Mexico and Central America.

FAMOUS MUMMMIES

● **The Gebelein pre-dynastic mummies** form a group of six mummies discovered at the end of the 19th century at Gebelein, a town south of Thebes. These mummies have been dated to 3400 BCE, making them the oldest Egyptian mummies ever found.

● **Hatshepsut's mummy** was not discovered in her tomb, but in the tomb of her nurse. It was found in 1903 CE, but only recently have medical tests confirmed it as the mummy of Hatshepsut.

● **The mummy of Thutmose II** was found in 1881 CE at Deir el-Medina. It had been badly damaged by tomb robbers who broke its left arm and chopped off the right arm.

● **Pharaoh Seqenenra Taa** died in battle and his mummy reflects the story of his death. It bears the wounds from an ax on its forehead and a dagger on its neck.

● **Akhenaten's mummy** was originally buried in his tomb at Akhetaten. After the city was abandoned, it was moved to tomb KV 55 in the Valley of the Kings, where it was discovered in 1907 CE.

● **The mummy of Tutankhamun** was found intact in its sarcophagus in 1924 CE. Medical tests performed on the mummy have shown that the young pharaoh was suffering from malaria when he died.

● When tomb robbers broke into the tomb of **Seti I**, they cut off the mummy's head. A priest of Amun reattached the head using linen strips.

In 1974, the mummy of Ramesses II was flown to Paris. It was given a passport in which his occupation was listed as King (Deceased).

● **Ramesses II was mummified in** 1213 BCE. Hieroglyphs on the outer wrappings tell us that the mummy was originally buried in his tomb, KV 7, but was moved to the tomb of his queen Inhapy for fear of tomb robbers. After 72 hours, it was moved again to the tomb of a high priest named Pinudjem II, where it was eventually found.

● **The mummy of Iufaa,** an Egyptian high priestess, was discovered in 1998 CE in a tomb at Abusir. Archeologists were delighted because the tomb had not been broken into, and Iufaa's mummy and grave goods were still intact.

Egypt at a glance

DAILY LIFE

★ **Rich people** had houses in towns, as well as villas in rural areas. Villas could have up to 70 rooms, including servant quarters.

★ **The father** was the head of the family, and the oldest son, the heir. However, women could do business and own property.

★ **Egyptian girls** could be married by the time they were 12 years old. Boys were married by the age of 15.

★ **Egyptians ate a balanced diet,** with vegetables, bread, legumes, meat, and dairy products.

HUNTING

• **Wildlife** in and around the Nile included fish, birds, crocodiles, and hippopotamuses. Animals such as jackals, lions, and antelope came to drink at the river.

• **Dangerous beasts,** such as hippopotamuses, were hunted using spears and lassoes.

• **Fast-moving animals,** such as hares and antelope, were hunted using bows and arrows.

MILITARY

▶ **In the Old Kingdom,** Egyptian soldiers carried a spear called a "kesh." Some soldiers had bows, shields, and short stabbing swords called metpenets.

▶ **During the New Kingdom,** the units of the army were named after gods such as Ra and Amun.

▶ **Egyptian military ships** carried a square sail, but were mainly powered by oars.

▶ **In times of peace,** soldiers did civil work—quarrying stone, digging irrigation trenches, and building pyramids.

ART

★ **In portrait painting,** artists followed strict rules. Most of the body was shown facing sideways, but the eyes, shoulders, and chest were drawn facing the front.

★ **Egyptian paints** were made from natural material, such as minerals. Black paint was made from charcoal, white from chalk, red from iron oxide, and blue from copper or lapis lazuli.

FASHION

◆ **At banquets,** women wore cones of perfumed oil on top of their wigs. The oil melted in the heat and ran down their clothes. Perfumed oils were also used by nobles in their daily baths.

◆ **Men wore kilts,** and women wore simple tunics or dresses with shoulder straps.

TRADE

◆ **The Egyptians did not use money.** Instead, they exchanged goods and services for products or work. This practice is known as bartering.

◆ **Goods were valued** according to a standard weight of copper called a deben. For example, a goat worth four deben might be traded for four deben's worth of grain.

◆ **A deben weighed** around 30 oz (91 g). A smaller weight, called a kite, was used for more valuable goods, such as silver and gold.

◆ **Egyptian traders** exchanged crops, minerals, papyrus, and wine for luxury goods, such as wood, horses, and leopard skins.

THE CALENDAR

• **The ancient Egyptians were the first people** to divide the day into 24 hours. Their year had 360 days divided into 12 months, with five extra days at the end of the year.

• **A workman's week** was nine days long—the 10th day was a day of rest.

• **The farming year** was divided into three seasons: *Akhet,* the time in which the Nile River flooded; *Peret,* the season in which crops were planted; and *Shemu,* the time of harvest.

• **There were no official holidays** in ancient Egypt. However, people did not work on religious festivals. In later times, these took up one-third of the year, so some people took a lot of time off work.

Ancient Egyptians believed that the Nile River flowed through the center of Earth.

Hieroglyphs

The word "hieroglyph" comes from the Greek language and means "sacred symbol." Ancient Egyptians used hieroglyphs for writing both words and numbers.

ALPHABET

The Egyptian hieroglyphic writing system used hundreds of symbols that stood for whole words. They also used a smaller number of symbols that stood for sounds, as shown below, and could be used to spell out words like an alphabet.

Symbol	Object	Sounds like	Symbol	Object	Sounds like
	Quail	O in "soon"; U in "under"; W in "wick"		Twisted flax	H in "ich"
	Cow's belly	"Th" in "three"		Unknown	"Th" in "that"
	Reed leaf	Y in "young"; I in "ink" and "kite"		Water	N in "not"
	Snake	J in "junk" and "gin"		Hand	D in "dog"
	Loaf of bread	T in "top"		Owl	M in "man"
	Leg	B in "boat"		Horned viper	F in "foot"; V in "viper"
	Pot stand	G in "gap"		Hill	Q in "queen"

Symbol	Object	Sounds like
	Mat	P in "pet"
	Reed hut	H in "hut"
	Mouth	R in "right"
	Arm	A in "may"
	Vulture	A in "water"
	Door bolt	Z in "zebra"
	Tethering rope	"Ch" in "chip"
	Folded cloth	"Ss" in "glass"
	Pond	"Sh" in "show"
	Basket	K in "basket"

NUMBERS

The Egyptian counting system was based on the number 10, with different symbols for 1, 10, 100, and so on. To represent the number 27, for example, two symbols for 10, and seven for one were placed together.

Symbol	Number
	1
	10
	100
	1,000
	10,000
	100,000
	1,000,000

Glossary

Adze A tool used to cut and smooth wood.

Amulet A lucky charm, worn or carried to ward off evil.

Ancient Egypt The period between 3100 and 30 BCE, when Egypt was ruled by pharaohs.

Ankh The ancient Egyptian symbol for life. Only gods and royalty could wear or carry it.

Artifact Any man-made object.

Ba The Egyptian idea of the human soul. The *Ba* was thought to live on after death. It was depicted as a bird with a human head.

Canopic jars Four jars used to hold the embalmed stomach, liver, intestines, and lungs of a mummy.

Capstone The topmost, finishing stone of a pyramid or wall.

Cartouche An oval shape enclosing a pharaoh's name in hieroglyphs.

Casing An outer layer of a building. It is made of smooth, fine stone.

Cataract A strong rush of water around rocks that blocks a river's flow. There are five cataracts on the Nile River. Of these, two are in Egypt.

Colossus A larger than life-sized statue, usually of a king. Colossi are often found outside temples.

Crook A royal symbol representing kingship. It was shaped as a hooked shepherd's staff.

Delta A triangular landform at the mouth of a river, formed by the settling out of silt and sand.

Demotic A script used in ancient Egypt, mainly for legal documents.

Dynasty A series of rulers from the same family. There were 31 dynasties during the history of ancient Egypt.

Duat The Egyptian underworld. People believed that the spirits of the dead traveled through *Duat* before being reborn in the afterlife.

Embalming The artificial preservation of a dead body using salts, perfumes, and ointments.

Faïence A glazed ceramic. In ancient Egypt, it was used to make jewelry and small statues.

False door A symbolic gateway carved or painted on tombs and coffins, through which a dead person's spirit was thought to pass.

First Intermediate Period (2160–2055 BCE) A time of division and unrest in Egypt after the Old Kingdom broke down.

Flail A tool to separate grain from plants. It was used in ancient Egypt as a symbol of the pharaoh's authority.

Hieroglyphics An ancient Egyptian system of writing in which pictures represented sounds, objects, and ideas.

Ka The Egyptian idea of the life-force of a person. It was shown as two raised hands.

Kohl Black eye make-up made from galena.

Lapis lazuli A bright blue semi-precious stone from Afghanistan. It was used in ancient Egyptian jewelry and also in other artifacts.

Late Period (664–332 BCE) The period of Egyptian history just before conquest by Alexander.

Lower Egypt The northern part of Egypt.

Mastaba A type of early Egyptian tomb, made of Sun-dried mud bricks and stone. It was rectangular, with low, sloping slides and a flat roof.

Middle Kingdom (2055–1650 BCE) The second main period of calm in Egyptian history, when Egypt was united under one pharaoh.

Mortuary temple A building next to the pyramid or tomb of a pharaoh. Since pharaohs were believed to become gods after death, these buildings were used as temples for their worship.

Mummy A dead body that has been preserved from decay, either naturally or by artificial means.

New Kingdom (1550–1069 BCE) The third main period of stability and achievement in Egyptian history, when Egypt was united under one pharaoh.

Nemes A headdress worn by an Egyptian pharaoh and often found on representations of the king.

Nomen The name given to a pharaoh when he or she was born.

belisk A tall stone
olumn with a square
r rectangular base
nd sloping sides
sing to a pointed tip.
belisks were erected
y pharaohs to celebrate
heir victories, or to
onor someone.

bsidian A glassy
ock formed from
olidified lava, used
or decoration and as a
nirror. Because obsidian
orms a very sharp edge
when it breaks, it was
lso used to make
utting tools.

ld Kingdom
2686–2180 BCE) The
rst major period of
chievement and
tability in Egyptian
istory, when Egypt
was united under one
haraoh and the great
yramids were built.

Oracle A priest or
eligious person who
was believed to be able
o communicate with
he gods.

Papyrus A type of paper
made from papyrus reeds.

Pectoral A piece of
ewelry that was worn
on the chest.

Pharaoh The title
given to the rulers of
ancient Egypt. The word
pharaoh means "great
nouse," and originally
eferred to the palace
ather than the ruler.

Praenomen A name
taken by a pharaoh after
being crowned. It referred
to the eternal kingship of
the pharaohs.

Ptolemaic Period
(332 BCE–30 BCE) The
final period of ancient
Egyptian history, when
Egypt was ruled by Greeks
descended from the first
Greek ruler, Ptolemy I.

Pylon The entrance
wall of a temple.

Pyramid A massive
stone structure with a
square base and four
sloping sides, which
could be either straight
or stepped. In ancient
Egypt, pyramids were
built as tombs
for pharaohs.

Pyramidion The
capstone of a pyramid.
These are sometimes
inscribed with the name
and image of the owner.

Pyramid texts Religious
writings carved on the
walls inside a pyramid.
These were a collection
of spells to help the dead
pharaoh reach the afterlife.

Relief A carved
or molded sculpture
that stands out from
its background.

Sarcophagus A stone
coffin that is either
rectangular or human-
shaped. The word means
"flesh-eater" in Greek.

Scarab An Egyptian dung
beetle. It was seen as a
symbol of the rising Sun.

Scribe An official
record-keeper who,
unlike most ordinary
people, could read
and write. Scribes had a
high status in society.

**Second Intermediate
Period** (1650–1550 BCE)
A time of division and
unrest in Egypt after the
Middle Kingdom. Asian
invaders called the
Hyksos controlled
parts of Egypt.

Shemayat A title given
to female musicians who
played in temples.

Soul house A miniature
model house placed in
the tomb of its dead
owner for his or her
use in the afterlife.

Sphinx A mythological
creature with a lion's
body and a human's
head. Statues of
sphinxes were
sometimes given the
head of a ram. These
were called criosphinxes.

Stela An upright stone
slab or pillar covered with
carvings or inscriptions.

**Third Intermediate
Period** (1069–664 BCE)
A time of instability when
Egypt was divided after
the New Kingdom broke
down, and was partly
ruled, at times, by Nubia.

Tomb A grave,
monument, or building
where the body of a
dead person is laid
to rest.

Upper Egypt The
southern part of Egypt.

Uraeus A cobra-shaped
carving associated with
the snake-headed
goddess Wadjet. It was
thought to protect the
pharaoh by spitting fire
at his or her enemies.

Valley of the Kings
A valley on the western
bank of the Nile River
near Thebes. It contains
the tombs of many
New Kingdom pharaohs.

Wadjet eye
A protective symbol
widely used in ancient
Egypt. It represented
the eye of the sky
god Horus and was
also known as the
eye of Horus.

Index

AB

Abu Simbel 5, 99
Abusir 46–7, 50
Abydos 5, 87
acrobats 143
adzes 136
aegis 106
afterlife 41, 60, 80–1
Ahmose I 8
Akhenaten 19, 30, 76, 145
alabaster sphinx of
  Memphis 69
Alexander the Great 9, 35
alphabet 148–9
Amada, Temple of 103
Amasis 34–5
Amenemhat I 24
Amenemhat II 25
Amenemhat III 51
  Pyramid of 144
Amenhotep II 30
  tomb of 57
Amenhotep III, tomb of 56
Ammut 80, 81
amulets 75, 81, 134–5
Amun/Amun-Ra 76, 93
ancient Egyptians 16–39
animal cults 79
Ankhesenamun, Queen
  16, 17, 67
Anubis 79, 80, 81, 86–7,
  97
Apep 94–5
Apis Bull 79, 109
arrows 127
Arsinoe I 36
Arsinoe III 37
art 146

artificial toe 134
Aswan 5, 105
Aten 76, 95
  Small temple of 105
Atum 77, 84–5
axes 136
Ay, tomb of 58
ba 80
baboon statue 70
balls, painted 123
barter 147
basalt 45
Bastet 94
Bent Pyramid 48, 144
Berenice II 37
Bes 95
Black Pyramid 51
board games 114, 120–1
boats 132–3
bow drills 137
bracelet of Nimlot 138
bread 116, 117
building materials 44–5
building tools 42–3, 136–7

CD

calendar 147
canopic chests 41
canopic jars 64–5, 81
canopic shrines 64–5
carpenters 114
cartouches 17
cat mummy 109
cat, wooden 122
cattle 130–1
chariots 12–13
chisels 137
clappers 125

Cleopatra VII 9, 37
Cleopatra's Needle 71
clothes and cloth 114,
  118–19, 147
Colossi of Memnon 69
copper standard 107
corn mummy 108
cosmetic jars 140–1
craftworkers 18, 114, 138
Criosphinx 70–1
crocodile mummy 108–9
crops 128
daily life 112–43, 146
Dakka, Temple of 100–1
dancers 143
Darius I the Great 35
Dashur 48–9, 51
dates 117
deben 147
Deir el-Shelwit 104
demotic script 11
Dendera 104
Derr, Temple of 102
Djed amulet 134
Djoser 20, 51
doctors 134
dogs and jackals 122
dolls, wooden 123
drills 137
Duamutef 65
Duat 80

EF

Early Dynastic Period 6
earrings 66, 139
Ennead 77, 84–5
eye makeup 140–1
falcons 8, 77, 107, 138

Acknowledgments

...rling Kindersley would like to thank:
...rie Mack for proofreading and Helen Peters
...indexing.

...e publisher would like to thank the following
... their kind permission to reproduce
...eir photographs:

...ey: a-above; b-below/bottom; c-center; f-far;
...ft; r-right; t-top)

...Corbis: Sandro Vannini (cl). 2-3 Getty Images:
...n McKinnell / Taxi (c). 3 Getty Images: J. D.
...allet / age fotostock (tr). 4 Getty Images: DEA
... Dagli Orti (tc); Grant Faint / Digital Vision (b).
...5 Getty Images: Michael Ochmeling. 5 Alamy
...mages: WildViews / Charles Tomalin (bl). Getty
...ages: Stephen Studd / Photographer's Choice
...(cl). 6 Corbis: Gianni Dagli Orti (bl). Dorling
...indersley: The Trustees of the British Museum
...(b). 6-7 Getty Images: DEA / A. Vorgani (bc). 7
...lamy Images: The Print Collector (tl). Corbis:
...werner Forman (tr). 8 Getty Images: Egyptian
...5th Dynasty / The Bridgeman Art Library (hr).
...Jürgen Liepe: (cl). 8-9 Getty Images: Niels van

Gijn / AWL Images (w). 9 Corbis: Ocean (bc).
Getty Images: DEA / G. Dagli Orti (cra). 10
Dorling Kindersley: The Trustees of the British
Museum (ch, bl). 10-11 Getty Images: DEA
Picture Library (tc, c, ca). 12 Jürgen Liepe: (c). 12-13
Getty Images: DEA / G. Dagli Orti (c). 13 Dorling Kindersley:
The Trustees of the British Museum (tl, tr / Short
Sword). Jürgen Liepe: (tr). 14-15 Getty Images:
12th Dynasty Egyptian / The Bridgeman Art
Library (l). 16 Getty Images: Sandro Vannini (bl).
19 Alamy Images: Egyptian,
5th Dynasty (c.2494-2345 BC) / The Art Gallery
Collection (br). Getty Images: Andreas Rentz (tr).
20 Alamy Images: Interfoto / Personalities (cl).
Corbis: Alfredo Dagli Orti / The Art Archive (bc);
Roger Wood (bl). Getty Images: DEA / A. Dagli
Orti / De Agostini (tl). 21 Getty Images: Egyptian /
The Bridgeman Art Library (l). Jürgen Liepe: (br).
22 Corbis: Alfredo Dagli Orti / The Art Archive (l).
Getty Images: DEA / S. Vannini (tr). 22-23 Alamy
Picture Library (t). 22-23 Alamy Images:
INTERFOTO / Fine Arts (bc). 23 Alamy Images:
Ian M Butterfield (Egypt) (br). Getty Images:

Leemage / Universal Images Group (tl). 24 Alamy
Images: Peter Horree (cra); Getty Images:
Leemage / Universal Images Group (l). 25 Alamy
Images: Art Media / The Print Collector (cr);
Hans Steen / dieKleinert (br). Getty Images:
12th Dynasty Egyptian / The Bridgeman Art
Library (l). 26 Corbis: Blainé Harington III /
Egyptian Museum, Cairo (cra). Getty Images:
Dea Picture Library / De Agostini Picture Library
(c). 26-27 Getty Images: Patrick Landmann (bc).
27 Corbis: Charles and Josette Lenars (tl). Getty
Images: DEA / G. Dagli Orti / De Agostini Picture
Library (br). 28-29 Getty Images: Dea / A. Dagli
Orti / De Agostini (c). 30 The Art Archive: Gianni
Dagli Orti / Musée du Louvre Paris (cb). Getty
Images: DEA / G. Dagli Orti / De Agostini Picture
Library (b). 31 Getty Images: Sean Gallup. 32
Getty Images: Hisham Ibrahim / Photographer's
Choice (tc). 32-33 Alamy Images: Peter Horree
(tc). Getty Images: DEA / A. Jemolo / De
Agostini Picture Library (bc). 33 The Art Archive:
Jacqueline Hyde / British Museum (br). 34
Corbis: Roger Wood (c). Getty Images: DEA /
A. Dagli Orti / De Agostini Picture Library (cl).
34-35 Corbis: Araldo de Luca (bc). 35 Corbis: